AI FOR UNDERSTANDING HUMAN CONVERSATIONS

Artificial intelligence (AI) and specifically large language models (LLMs) revolutionize our lives with new technologies appearing at an unprecedented rate. These technologies can potentially change how we understand human conversations, from the dialogues of married couples to diplomatic conversations.

This book explains how to use LLMs to analyze human conversations and how better LLMs can be developed by incorporating a deep theoretical understanding.

Drawing on case studies from Pulp Fiction to diplomatic meetings, the book provides detailed, approachable, and theoretically grounded explanations of how LLMs can help us understand conversations.

Prof. Yair Neuman is the head of the Functor Lab at Ben-Gurion University of the Negev, Israel. He is the author of several books published by leading publishers and has been a visiting Prof. at universities such as MIT and Oxford. He is a leading authority in using AI for psychology, social sciences, and the humanities, and DARPA has sponsored his recent research.

AI FOR EVERYTHING

Artificial intelligence (AI) is all around us. From driverless cars to game winning computers to fraud protection, AI is already involved in many aspects of life, and its impact will only continue to grow in future. Many of the world's most valuable companies are investing heavily in AI research and development, and not a day goes by without news of cutting-edge breakthroughs in AI and robotics.

The *AI for Everything* series explores the role of AI in contemporary life, from cars and aircraft to medicine, education, fashion and beyond. Concise and accessible, each book is written by an expert in the field and will bring the study and reality of AI to a broad readership including interested professionals, students, researchers, and lay readers.

AI for Sports
Chris Brady, Karl Tuyls, Shayegan Omidshafiei

AI for Learning
Carmel Kent & Benedict du Boulay

AI for the Sustainable Development Goals
Henrik Skaug Sætra

AI for School Teachers
Rose Luckin. Karine George & Mutlu Cukurova

AI for Healthcare Robotics
Eduard Fosch-Villaronga & Hadassah Drukarch

AI for Physics
Volker Knecht

AI for Diversity
Roger A. Søraa

AI for Finance
Edward P. K. Tsang

AI for Communication
David J. Gunkel

AI for Scientific Discovery
Janna Hastings

AI for Peace
Branka Panic Paige Arthur

AI for Understanding Human Conversations
Yair Neuman

For more information about this series please visit:
https://www.routledge.com/AI-for-Everything/book-series/AIFE

AI FOR UNDERSTANDING HUMAN CONVERSATIONS

YAIR NEUMAN

CRC Press
Taylor & Francis Group
Boca Raton London New York

CRC Press is an imprint of the
Taylor & Francis Group, an **informa** business

Designed cover image: Shutterstock_2341886709

First edition published 2025
by CRC Press
2385 NW Executive Center Drive, Suite 320, Boca Raton FL 33431

and by CRC Press
4 Park Square, Milton Park, Abingdon, Oxon, OX14 4RN

CRC Press is an imprint of Taylor & Francis Group, LLC

Library of Congress Cataloging-in-Publication Data
Names: Neuman, Yair, 1968- author.
Title: AI for understanding human conversations / Yair Neuman.
Other titles: Artificial intelligence for understanding human conversations
Description: First edition. | Boca Raton FL : CRC Press, 2025. | Series: AI
for everything | Includes bibliographical references and index. |
Identifiers: LCCN 2024046788 | ISBN 9781032968780 (hardback) |
ISBN 9781032968766 (paperback) | ISBN 9781003591047 (ebook)
Subjects: LCSH: Conversation analysis. | Artificial intelligence.
Classification: LCC P95.45 .N468 2025 | DDC 302.34/6028563--dc23/eng/20250118
LC record available at https://lccn.loc.gov/2024046788

ISBN: 9781032968780 (hbk)
ISBN: 9781032968766 (pbk)
ISBN: 9781003591047 (ebk)

DOI: 10.1201/9781003591047

Typeset in Joanna
by KnowledgeWorks Global Ltd.

CONTENTS

PREFACE

Every child grows to understand that human beings are talking creatures. We interact with each other primarily through language, the most powerful platform available to us to express our thoughts, wishes, and emotions, and we learn to do it from a very young age. However, realizing that human beings converse doesn't ease the challenge of understanding human conversations. But why should that be a challenge when we are socialized to participate in conversations from birth? The answer is that human conversations are multilayered and interactive, and they unfold in a nonlinear way. This means that: (1) a conversation may include several layers or levels of meaning; (2) by interacting with others, conversations result in wholes that differ from the sum of their parts; and (3) conversations evolve nonlinearly, which means that the progression of a conversation will not usually follow any simple and predictable path. The complexity of conversations includes additional factors such as the social frames of the participants, their mutual history and memories of past interactions, their unique individual perspectives, and the hidden unconscious layers of the individuals that are not available to outside observers. So, understanding a conversation is no trivial matter. It always requires a certain effort.

As explained half-jokingly by Bernard Shaw, "The single biggest problem in communication is the illusion that it has taken place." Indeed, the idea that we fully understand others who fully understand us is a repeated illusion in social interactions and a source of difficulties expressed in a wide range of contexts, from conversations between married couples to diplomatic meetings.

Traditionally, human conversations have been analyzed using 'soft' interpretative methodologies. I have been involved in this kind of analysis for over 20 years. However, the revolution introduced by AI, specifically large language models (LLMs), transforms the way we analyze and understand conversations. This revolution stems from the unique characteristics of LLMs. They are not dumb input–output machines but artificial minds performing in a remarkably similar way to human intelligence.

The revolution brought about by LLMs cannot be attributed to theories developed in linguistics, conversation analysis, or psycholinguistics. Surprising as it may sound, the most advanced artificial intelligence technology we use today has been developed with total disregard for the fields that traditionally study human intelligence (e.g., psychology) and language (e.g., linguistics). This doesn't mean that the use of LLMs cannot be inspired by theory. The book shows how these state-of-the-art AI technologies may transform our understanding of human conversations by incorporating theoretical approaches from various disciplines.

The book addresses two main audiences: those interested in understanding human conversations using AI in the form of LLMs and those who develop LLMs to understand human conversations. Such audiences usually have different backgrounds and would be approached in different ways. This book is an exception in that it addresses both audiences that could benefit significantly from this book with its theoretically grounded, practical, and interdisciplinary approach.

ACKNOWLEDGMENTS

I am grateful to Prof. Z. Bekerman, who introduced me to discourse and conversation analysis 25 years ago. I would like to thank Yochai Cohen for running the VPD code and Boaz Tamir for reviewing this measure.

1

HUMAN CONVERSATIONS AND THE PROMISE OF AI

INTRODUCTION

Conversation is "interactive communication between two or more people" (Wikipedia). Historically, the word 'conversation,' in the sense of the "informal interchange of *thoughts* and *sentiments* by spoken words" (my emphasis), appeared in the 16th century.[1] One should notice that the word conversation comprises the prefix 'con-' + 'versare.' The Latin prefix 'con-' means 'with' or 'together.' It is often used to indicate something that happens collectively or in partnership. Therefore, it is not surprising that 'conversation' was also used as a synonym for 'sexual intercourse.' Some activities, such as talking and sex, require partnership and interaction. This is an important point to understand. Conversations involve *interactions* mediated by sign systems (e.g., language, gestures, etc.). Therefore, conversations are systems comprised of interdependent and interactive components. Systems with interacting and dependent components are known to be a source of complexity (Bak, 2013), and human conversations are no exception. Thus, we need an appropriate set of theoretical and technological tools to understand a conversation as a complex system.

The second component of the word conversation is 'versare,' which originates from 'vertere.' As a verb, the Latin word 'vertere' means

DOI: 10.1201/9781003591047-1

'to cause to revolve or move about a centre.'[2] Combining 'con' and 'versare' gives the word 'conversation' a sense of 'turning together' around a topic. Therefore, conversation is a sign-mediated interaction/ communication revolving around an issue. It is not always clear what the issue is. When conversing, people may discuss different topics, and sometimes the real issue is not the topic but the group dynamics or unconscious and hidden streams flowing underneath the surface.

THE CHALLENGE OF ANALYZING CONVERSATIONS

What is required to participate in conversations and understand them? The simple answer is socialization. From an early age, we learn to take part in conversations. However, 'socialization' is such a broad term that it is almost uninformative. Participating in a conversation requires many skills, from understanding the language to social dynamics, turn-taking, shifts in topic, and sociocultural nuances. Moreover, understanding the deep layers of a conversation requires more than we are usually able to achieve through socialization. Here is a simple example illustrating the complexity of understanding a relatively simple slice of a conversation.

The slice of conversation that I analyze is taken from Tarantino's famous film *Pulp Fiction*.[3] For some, the film is difficult to digest as it involves a strange mixture of violence, humor, 'street philosophy,' trash talk, and repulsive scenes. The characters are grotesque and sometimes seem like comic figures rather than real humans. At the same time, they are deeply human and involved in moral and philosophical conversations that do not seem to correspond to their grotesque character and behavior.

The opening scene of the movie takes place in an American diner. As presented in the movie script, the context is as follows:

1. Coffee shop.
2. Morning (9:00).
3. A normal Denny's, Spires-like coffee shop in Los Angeles.

4. The place isn't jammed.
5. A healthy number of people drinking coffee, munching on bacon, and eating eggs.

This context will appear visually in the mind's eye of those who have seen the movie. It is also the context where we first meet a young man and a young woman conversing. To understand the context as the backdrop of the conversation, we must have some *background knowledge*. For example, we should know that Denny's is a famous American diner-style restaurant chain that is open 24/7. 'Spires-like' refers to a specific style of coffee shops and diners that were once common in Southern California. Spires was a chain of coffee shops known for their distinctive mid-century modern architecture, often featuring a sharp, upward-pointing 'spire' as part of their design. These coffee shops were similar in style and atmosphere to Denny's, offering a *casual* and *accessible* dining experience. So, when the script describes the coffee shop as 'a normal Denny's, Spires-like coffee shop,' it's conveying the idea of a typical, unremarkable, and familiar diner setting in Los Angeles, with a style reminiscent of these classic, mid-century diners.

Why do we need background knowledge? The answer is simple. Background knowledge *frames* our understanding of the conversation. It helps us *interpret* the situation, develop *expectations*, and identify *anomalies*. This is an important point. Please keep it in mind to frame your reading of the book.

The context, visually presented to the audience in the opening scene, evokes a sense of ordinariness and familiarity. To understand the context, as described in the opening of the movie script, we should also understand the meaning of 'munching.' 'Munching' refers to eating something enthusiastic or enjoyable, often with noticeable chewing sounds. When the script says that people are munching bacon, it means they are eating bacon in a way that suggests they are enjoying it, perhaps taking bites that involve a bit of chewing, which might be audible. Hearing people eating is a clear sign of social class. Therefore, even describing people as munching is an informative sign, as it tells us something about the people eating and the atmosphere of the place.

The context described in the script's opening sets the initial frame for understanding the behavior and conversations of people who visit the diner. To better understand the frame, I asked ChatGPT to describe the ambiance of such a place, and it described it as follows (my emphasis):

> In this context, the ambiance of the coffee shop can be described as *relaxed* and familiar, with a touch of early morning energy. The place has a *comforting, everyday* feel, with the scent of freshly brewed coffee mingling with the savory aroma of bacon and eggs. The clientele is likely a mix of regulars and passersby, giving the shop a *cozy, communal* vibe. The background noise is a gentle hum of low conversation, the clinking of cutlery, and the occasional hiss of the coffee machine. The lighting is probably soft and natural, with sunlight streaming through the windows, adding to the warmth and inviting atmosphere. The overall mood is *comfort* and *routine*, where people start their day in a *familiar, unhurried* environment.

In this context, requiring some background knowledge, we meet a conversing couple described in the script as a young man and a young woman. The young man opens by saying: "No, forget it, it's too risky. I'm through doin' that shit." Notice how much we can learn even by paying attention to the words used in this utterance. For example, using the word 'shit' is indicative of the speaker, his 'stance,' and the 'frame' of the conversation. The word 'shit' is considered vulgar and is typically avoided in formal or polite conversation. Its use is more common in casual, informal contexts, often among people comfortable with each other or in settings where rougher language is acceptable. Here we are in an LA coffee shop, probably frequented by low- to middle-class Americans, enjoying their breakfast in a relaxing atmosphere. A couple is conversing, and one uses a vulgar word. Therefore, to understand the conversation, we must also understand the metaphorical and vulgar use of 'shit' and its role in the social dynamics of the participants. This implies that understanding a conversation involves some background knowledge about the use of language and the way it informs us about the speakers. Conversely, the way people talk with each other informs us about the speakers, their stance, and the frame of the conversation. For instance, assume you know nothing about the context in which the word 'shit' has been used. Now, I ask you to guess in which context it is more likely that the word has been produced: (1) two lower middle-class Americans in a diner or (2) two theoretical physicists during a lunch break? You will probably guess right, and your correct guess is based on an unconscious and automatic understanding of language with its informative signs.

The conversation between the two opens as follows:

Young man:	No, forget it, it's too risky. I'm through doin' that shit.
Young woman:	You always say that, the same things every time: never again, I'm through, too dangerous.
Young man:	I know that's what I always say. I'm always right too, but ...
Young woman:	... but you forget about it in a day or two.

What happens in this opening slice of the conversation? From a naïve perspective, it seems rather trivial. There's no meat on the bone. The participants seemed to understand each other as the conversation flowed easily with no questions (e.g., what do you mean?) or requests for explanation. However, the challenge for us, as outside observers, is much greater. When developing a system for analyzing human conversations or when using large language models (LLMs) to understand human conversation, we shift our stance from active participants to active, albeit external analysts.

To understand the conversation, we must use some theoretical constructs that may help us to frame the conversation. This means we must use some tools to help us make sense of the conversation.

Interestingly, most concepts and ideas developed in conversation or discourse analysis have no relevance to the era of LLMs. I have been analyzing human discourse for over a decade (e.g., Neuman et al., 2002; Neuman & Levi, 2003; Neuman, 2013), but changing my focus to artificial intelligence (AI), I learned that very few of these ideas have stood the test of time. Most of the ideas that have survived deal with the pragmatics of language or the way meaning is formed in context.

The first construct I would like to use is the one known as a speech act. A speech act is an utterance that serves a function in communication, where the speaker performs an action through their words. Identifying the speech act expressed by an utterance directs us to the function of the utterance. For instance, the utterance: "I wish you were here now" expresses a directive speech act. This is one in which the speaker tries to get the listener to do something. This can involve giving commands, making requests, offering suggestions, or expressing wishes that imply a desire for the listener to take some action. The key feature of a directive is that it attempts to influence the behavior or actions of the listener. For instance, the utterance "I wish you would stay longer" asks the listener to stay longer, unless it is just used to be polite with no real intention for the listener to stay. In the latter, more complex context, the listener should not understand the utterance at face value and stay. The listener should be familiar with the frame of a polite visit, where the host expresses his 'wish' while actually seeking his visitor's polite refusal and departure. In Pink Floyd's 'Wish You Were Here,' the utterance seems to express a genuine wish. The singer longs for the addressee's presence. Clearly, our understanding is possible only through 'top-down' frames, which we use to interpret a conversation, and 'bottom-up' analysis of microlevel moves such as speech acts. In the context of a dinner party, the host may say to his departing guests, "Oh, I wish you could have stayed longer." Accepting his 'invitation' would be a misunderstanding. To understand the utterance, one must be equipped with the appropriate frame or context (Neuman, 2024).

In this book, I rely on this top-down and bottom-up approach. On the one hand, I seek to identify the general frame through which speakers' moves can be interpreted. On the other hand, I seek to understand the micro-moves, such as speech acts, that may inform us about the frame. Understanding conversations from one perspective alone, either from the top or the bottom, is an error that occurs repeatedly. The two perspectives are complimentary. Moreover, as taught in Bateson's seminal work (Harries-Jones, 1995), the top-down and bottom-up perspectives complement each other dynamically. When my host says: "I wish you could have stayed for another drink," I must try to understand whether his directive is intentional or results from a general frame of politeness. More cues are required to understand the situation.

Identifying the speech acts expressed in an utterance is a powerful tool for analyzing the conversation, and LLMs do remarkable work in identifying speech acts. To illustrate the explanatory power of speech acts, let us return to the coffee shop and the conversation between the young man and woman. Watching the scene, we gain a significant amount of information that serves as a context for interpretation. The way these people look, their tone, how they hold their cigarettes, and so on, are highly informative. When developing AI agents to understand a conversation, we should adopt a multimodal approach, where all types of information are gathered, analyzed, and merged. However, for the limited purpose of this book, I will focus only on what the speakers say, as if I hadn't seen the movie.

In the first utterance, the young man uses the speech act of *assertion*. He asserts his decision to stop engaging in a risky activity, emphasizing that he's finished with it. From this assertion, we may infer that the young man has been involved in a risky activity and has decided to make a change and stop doing so. Even by analyzing the opening utterance of the conversation, we may gain a significant amount of information:

1. The young man uses a vulgar term, hinting at his background.
2. He was involved in risky activity.
3. He has decided to make a change and stop this involvement in the risky activity.

However, the assertion is functional. It aims to achieve something with respect to the *addressee* of the utterance. Utterances cannot be analyzed in a vacuum. Understanding that utterances are generated in an interaction, we should always ask which addressee is targeted and why. What communicative function is achieved through the assertion generated by the young man? Although we cannot get into his mind, we can generate wise hypotheses or guesses. Therefore, when using and developing LLMs to understand conversations, we must use a *reasoning* component trained specifically in the social context of conversations. This is not a matter of logical reasoning. It is reasoning through the probabilistic and context-sensitive process of hypothesis generation and hypothesis testing.

One possible function of the abovementioned assertion may be to convince the young woman to agree or at least understand his decision. Here, we may hypothesize that the young woman is asking him to do something risky. To the above information, we may add the following hypotheses:

1. The young man is trying to convince the young woman to agree with his decision.
2. The young woman is asking the young man to do something risky.

The generation of hypotheses is built into our understanding of a conversation. Testing these hypotheses is a way of validating our understanding, testing our frames, and supporting our interpretations. If the hypothesis that the man is trying to convince the woman to agree with his decision is correct, we should see it in her *response*. Here is another important layer that I would like to add to our understanding. As explained by Michal Holquist, "Nothing means anything until it achieves a response" (Holquist, 1990, p. 48). Holquist's argument is very important. If meaning exists in response, then understanding the meaning of an utterance or a conversation is possible only by analyzing the dynamics of utterances and responses in an interaction. This highly important theoretical approach may guide our use of LLMs.

What can be expected from the response of the young woman? Understanding a conversation involves the active role of the participants, who draw inferences and form expectations. The young woman may agree or disagree with the young man. The young woman's response ("You always say that …") expresses the speech act of criticism, accusation, or complaint. She complains about his repetitive behavior, highlighting his inconsistency and the fact that he always makes the same declarations. First, we can see that her response does not align with the man's decision. Her response validates the hypothesis that the man was asking for the woman's approval or support for his decision. However, he didn't get it.

What is the function of the woman's criticism? To change the young man's mind? To express her superior stance with respect to him? In response to the young woman's criticism, the young man uses the speech act of concession. He is conceding or acknowledging the truth of the woman's statement, admitting that he always says the same thing. The woman responds with the speech act of reproach, as she is reproaching the young man for his inconsistency, pointing out that he quickly forgets his decisions.

As we can see, this thin opening slice of the conversation involves several layers of meaning that may be excavated through a careful theoretically grounded analysis. For example, the young man tries to express assertiveness and authority, but the woman challenges his authority by pointing out his inconsistency. Therefore, identifying the speech acts may be the first step in exposing the conversation dynamics and the relationship between the speakers.

We may also learn about the speakers' personalities by analyzing the utterances. Admitting his repetitive pattern, the young man exposes his vulnerability. His somewhat manly way of speaking ("I'm through doin' that shit") seems to be an attempt to look tough rather than genuine toughness. This point can be deepened through Goffman's idea of the *face* (Goffman, 1955). Goffman used 'face' to refer to the positive social value a person claims for themselves in a given interaction. It's about maintaining a certain self-image or reputation in the eyes of others, which is often done by managing how one presents oneself in social situations. This idea is echoed in a modern theory of social emotions, where the function of social emotions, such as shame, is discussed in terms of social *valuation* (Sznycer & Lukaszewski, 2019). It is argued that the basic aspect of social interactions is valuing others and presenting one's value to others. A person known in their community as trustworthy presents a valuable trait to others, who can count on them for collaborative activities that may support their survival and well-being. In this context, social emotions are described as tools for supporting this valuation system. For example, a person presenting his achievements may present them with pride: "The pride system is designed to motivate the achievement and advertisement of socially valued acts or traits so that others place more weight on the individual's welfare" (Sznycer & Lukaszewski, 2019, p. 396). An important aspect of understanding a conversation is, therefore, the self as presented to others, or the *stance* presented by the individual.

The young man attempts to present himself as assertive, decisive, and determined. By saying that he's "through doin' that shit," he is trying to assert a face that is determined. The young woman's response is a *face-threatening act*. By pointing out that he "always says" the same things but doesn't follow through, she is threatening his desired self-image of being decisive. She undermines his social value by pointing out that he doesn't stand for his own words. Calling out the discrepancy between his words and actions undermines the face he is trying to maintain. As we now see, understanding this short and 'thin' slice of conversation is no trivial challenge as it involves several layers of meaning.

THE PRAGMATICS OF UNDERSTANDING CONVERSATIONS

At a certain point, we understand that the young man and woman are planning to rob the coffee shop. They use guns and threaten the clients and the employees. Imagine that you are a law enforcement officer arriving at the crime scene. What is the best way to negotiate with the young man and woman? Is there a way to convince them to surrender? The only data that you have is the above thin slice of conversation. The meaning of this conversation is the information you may extract and put to practical use to reduce the uncertainty involved in approaching these two young criminals. Imagine that you are the head of the LAPD SWAT team. In this case, you are not trained to analyze the conversation and probably have no idea how to improve your stance. Despite the fact that you have been involved in conversations most of your life, you have no expertise in analyzing this conversation. Imagine that you are the chief linguist of the LAPD SWAT team. You are probably clueless if you are a linguist trained in the Chomsky tradition. You may identify the grammatical structure of the utterances or even, inspired by your guru's political opinions, explain that the event results from the repressive capitalistic system. But there's nothing helpful there.

The only thing that can help us is understanding the conversation's meaning. At this point, we understand that the 'meaning of meaning' is the same as the proof of the pudding: it is in the taste. It means that our pudding is tasteless unless we analyze the conversation in such a way as to reduce uncertainty and support some action. Let me repeat this important point. Understanding the meaning of a conversation is not a challenge for the post-modernist who believes that 'anything goes,' or for the ideologically biased individual forcing his own interpretation on it. The value of the analysis is only in reducing uncertainty and supporting action. In other words, the taste of the pudding may be significantly improved if we are ready to adopt a pragmatic approach, such as the one presented in the above analysis. For instance, adopting the outcome of the above analysis, we learn something interesting about the young man and woman and their relationship. The young man presents himself as the 'man,' but he is actually conflictual and vulnerable. Regarding the power dynamics, the woman is the one in charge. If you want to control the situation, you should play on the young man's conflicts and vulnerability and the dominance of the young woman.

What can we learn so far? First, conversations are much more complex than may be naively assumed. While people may fluently participate in a conversation, understanding conversations from a reflective and analytical stance is much more difficult. The second thing we learn is that meaning is the kernel of human conversations. Extracting the meaning from utterances and conversations means we can represent them appropriately. From these representations, we can draw inferences that optimally support our actions, which means gaining a better understanding of the participants and their dynamics and forming predictions about the participant's future moves. The third point is that conversations are always contextual. This means that, in order to understand a conversation, we must incorporate it in a general scheme or frame that guides our analysis while paying attention to the particularities and nuances of the conversation. To better understand a conversation, we may use the revolutionary AI technology of LLMs.

THE PROMISE OF LLMs

LLMs are AI technologies designed for the sophisticated processing of text sequences. They are built using deep learning techniques, and in particular, deep neural networks with numerous parameters. These networks have been trained on vast amounts of text data to form a powerful 'model' of language. Such models learn patterns, context, and nuances in language, allowing them to perform tasks ranging from intelligent search[4] to creative writing. You may consult (Neuman et al., 2022) for a friendly exposition of these technologies. I highly recommend the 3Blue1Brown series on neural networks for a deeper understanding.[5] Here, I shall briefly present several important ideas that comprise the magic soup of LLM technology: embeddings, transformers, attention, context, and reasoning. So, let me explain them.

One crucial aspect of LLMs is the way they represent a text, whether a conversation or a novel. The text is broken into a sequence of tokens, and each token is represented as an array of numbers. Let me give you an oversimplified example that I use to explain the idea of LLMs to my students. It is an oversimplified example because the embeddings of OpenAI, which I use in this book, are produced differently and in a more sophisticated way.

Imagine reading the following sequence: "My favorite ice cream flavor is ...." As a part of the reading comprehension process, you try to guess the missing word. An appropriate sequence representation is necessary to support the guessing task, and the question is which representation to use. A long time ago, the cognitive psychologist Walter Kintsch suggested that representations could be modeled as propositions (Kintsch, 1998). Propositions are the smallest units of meaning. A proposition is essentially a simplified structure that captures the core idea of a sentence or phrase, often involving a relationship between concepts or entities. For example, the propositional representation of "I love banana" may include a *predicate-argument structure*: love (I, banana). This representation includes two arguments, 'I' and 'banana,' and one predicate, 'love.'

To represent the utterance "My favorite ice cream flavor is vanilla" using Kintsch's propositional representation, we would break it down into its core elements:

Predicate: favorite
Subject: I (implied by 'My')
Object: flavor
Attribute: vanilla
Relation: is

What happens if I ask ChatGPT to represent the utterance "My favorite ice cream flavor is …"? Here is what I get:

For the incomplete utterance, "My favorite ice-cream flavor is," the propositional representation would focus on the available information. Since the flavor is not specified, we can only represent the propositions that are clear from the utterance:

Predicate: favorite
Subject: I (implied by 'My')
Object: flavor
Relation: is (though the attribute is missing)
The propositional structure could be represented as:
Favorite (I, flavor)

The model adds the following explanation:

> This proposition represents that the speaker has a favorite ice cream flavor, but the corresponding attribute proposition is absent since the flavor itself is not provided. This reflects that the utterance is incomplete and lacks the specific information that normally follows the relation 'is.' The representation stops at what has been communicated, which is the existence of a favorite flavor, without specifying what it is.

The model correctly explains a basic problem of the propositional representation: it describes what there is and has no way of completing the sequence. It cannot predict the next word in the sequence. However, suppose we represent each word in the sequence through its accompanying words in a large corpus of texts. Let me explain this point by focusing on two words: 'flavor' and 'ice cream.' By analyzing a huge repository of texts, we may find that 'ice cream' is accompanied by words such as 'cone,' 'sundae,' 'chocolate,' and 'vanilla,' and that 'flavor' is accompanied by words such as 'sweet,' 'nutty,' 'smoky,' and 'delicate.' We may also find that 'chocolate' is more strongly associated with 'ice cream' than with 'flavor.'

Here, we represent the meaning of the two words, 'ice cream' and 'flavor,' by deciding on a predefined set of words and the extent to which they are associated with our target words. The words are 'cone,' 'sundae,' 'chocolate,' 'vanilla,' 'sweet,' 'nutty,' 'smoky,' and 'delicate.' These words define the 'dimensionality' of our representation of the words, in the sense that the meaning of the words 'ice cream' and 'flavor' is represented by their embeddings or the vectors of words associated with them. The representation of the meanings of the words as embeddings can be visualized as in Table 1.1.

Therefore, the meaning of each isolated word is represented through an *array* of numbers, a *vector*. The way these vectors or

TABLE 1.1 Embeddings for 'Ice Cream' and 'Flavor'

DIMENSION	EMBEDDING FOR 'ICE CREAM'	EMBEDDING FOR 'FLAVOR'
Cone	0.85	0.30
Sundae	0.90	0.40
Chocolate	0.70	0.75
Vanilla	0.80	0.85
Sweet	0.95	0.90
Nutty	0.65	0.70
Smoky	0.30	0.60
Delicate	0.40	0.80

embeddings are generated is far more complicated (see, e.g., Neelakantan et al., 2022) than the didactic examples I used above. The example is only an example.

The second ingredient of an LLM is that it processes sequences: its *transformer* architecture and *self-attention* mechanism may revise the above representations by considering the existence of other words in a sequence. This means that the representation of each word is updated by the representations of other words in the sequence.

Transformers use self-attention to understand the relationships between words in a sequence. Unlike traditional embeddings, which assign *static* vectors to words regardless of context, the attention mechanism *adjusts* these embeddings on the basis of the surrounding words. In this way, the architecture underlying LLMs can adapt the meaning of each word in a sequence to the context in which it appears. So, for instance, the embeddings for 'ice cream' and 'flavor' would be influenced by the context provided by the words "My favorite" and "is …." In the sequence "My favorite ice cream flavor is …," the words 'ice cream' and 'flavor' are closely related and contextually bound. The self-attention

TABLE 1.2 The Revised Embedding of 'Flavor'

DIMENSION	EMBEDDING FOR 'FLAVOR'
Cone	0.30
Sundae	0.30
Chocolate	0.80
Vanilla	0.85
Sweet	0.70
Nutty	0.72
Smoky	0.20
Delicate	0.35

mechanism will detect this relationship and adjust the embeddings accordingly. The revised embedding of flavor is shown in Table 1.2.

You can see that some dimensions of 'flavor' have been emphasized, given the existence of 'ice cream' in the sequence. So, if you are interested in guessing the flavor in the sequence "My flavor ice cream flavor is ...," some words, such as 'chocolate' and 'vanilla,' are more probable than others.

The classical ways of representing meaning, such as the one proposed by Kintsch, cannot do this. Here, we get to the third idea I want to discuss: context. Previously, I explained how the attention mechanism adjusts its representation to the representations of the other words. What this mechanism actually expresses is context sensitivity. Imagine you hear your friend uttering the following:

1. My favorite ice cream flavor is ...
2. My favorite steak flavor is ...

In the first case, you will probably guess words like 'chocolate' and 'vanilla,' but when processing the second sequence, the guess will probably be words like 'smoky' or 'delicate.' When guessing, you take context into account. LLMs, as guessing machines, can do the same. They combine context sensitivity with reasoning. Let me illustrate this point by using an advanced model.

The most advanced model I currently use is GPT-4o. From now on, I will refer to it as "the model." It represents texts by taking a piece of text as an input (more accurately, a sequence of tokens) and representing it as a vector, an array of numbers. Hence, "an embedding is a vector representation of a piece of data (e.g., some text) that is meant to preserve aspects of its content and/or its meaning."[6] The most advanced embedding used by GPT-4o is 'text-embedding-3-large,' and it involves a very high dimensionality for representing a text. This means that the text is converted to a highly sophisticated numerical representation that can be used to process any text. Later, I will show you how to use this embedding to better understand a diplomatic conversation.

I asked GPT-4o to perform the guessing task for the flavor of ice cream or steak, and it responded as follows:

> Given the context of each utterance, here are my guesses for the masked word:
>
> "My favorite ice cream flavor is …"
>
> Likely guess: Vanilla (other possibilities could be chocolate, strawberry, etc.)
>
> "My favorite steak flavor is …"
>
> Likely guess: Pepper (other possibilities could be garlic, smoky, barbecue, etc.)

You can see that the model performs in a way that is remarkably similar to human beings. Changing only one word in the sequence changed the context, resulting in a different representation of each word's meaning and totally different guesses or predictions for the next word. The model's guessing machine is not easy to understand. In fact, given the architecture and dynamics of the model, we cannot explain even a simple reasoning process. 3Blue1Brown explains this in his chapter titled "How might LLMs store facts." Our ability to explain complex systems is extremely limited, even if they are systems designed by humans.

In sum, LLMs such as GPT-4o have a remarkable ability to represent text and process it contextually using their unique architecture and learning patterns over massive datasets. Moreover, they can reason/guess extremely well. This reasoning is difficult to explain in any simple way in terms of their architecture and dynamics. The impressive performance of LLMs may raise the question of whether they can replace the human expert in analyzing and understanding human conversations. My answer is not yet. There is a gap, and several steps should be taken to fulfill the promise of LLMs, at least in helping us to understand conversations.

HOW TO USE LLMs?

The problem of using LLMs to understand human conversations may be discussed under the theme of "The Two Cultures." Years ago, C.P. Snow argued that intellectual life in the Western world was divided into two distinct cultures: the sciences and the humanities. Today, he would probably add engineering in alliance with the sciences. People involved in engineering AI systems, such as software engineers, are usually indifferent and insensitive to the unique aspects of the materials they analyze. There are exceptions, of course, but the general 'stance' adopted by this culture is one of engineering a system rather than dwelling deeply on aspects of the subject matter they analyze. In contrast, people with expertise in analyzing human behavior, whether discursive or psychological, are usually indifferent to AI technologies and, in some cases, suspicious of or even hostile toward them. Years of working in the field have led me to meet both types. Once, I gave a talk to a group of senior psychologists about my work in computational personality analysis (see, e.g., Neuman & Cohen, 2024). The responses ranged from amused indifference to explicit hostility: "Do you believe that this tool can replace us?" This was an oft-repeated question, usually addressed in a sarcastic tone. Along similar lines, I have met people from computer science who were eager to adopt the new technologies but paid little or no attention to the meaning of the linguistic or behavioral data they analyzed. I once worked with a leading computer scientist on a project that required the analysis of highly complex linguistic phenomena. He tried to apply his full arsenal of machine-learning weapons, using them to analyze a huge set of 100,000 language features. His approach failed, as he wouldn't try to understand the complex linguistic phenomena we were analyzing. This highly intelligent person gave up, but I found the solution by investing time and effort in better understanding the phenomena themselves. Understanding your subject matter may be of great value. Working between these two cultures, I believe both types of audiences may benefit significantly from looking beyond their usual safe environment.

Before the main chapters, I want to highlight the approach used in this book. As the technology of LLMs changes very quickly, I avoid any detailed discussions of technological issues. The book is written with a clearly conceptual orientation. Moreover, I focus on detailed and in-depth analysis of conversations, showing how both the understanding of conversations can be improved and smarter LLMs can be designed. While technology may change rapidly, the ideas presented in this little book may hopefully last longer. A final comment concerns the materials I chose for illustration and their detailed analysis. I generally analyze conversations from movies such as Pulp Fiction, No Land for Old Men, and Night at the Opera. A very simple logic guides my choice. Movies are not only fun but also include conversations with indispensable didactic value. Therefore, I provide a detailed analysis of conversations from movies. Although this detailed analysis might sometimes seem tedious, I see no way of illustrating the power of LLMs without going into the details. One should not consider the detailed analysis of the conversations as representing a pedantic approach but rather as an exercise in attentional observation.

SUMMARY

- Conversations involve linguistic, discursive, social, and psychological factors. They are usually more complex than we tend to believe.

- Context is crucial in understanding conversations. LLMs excel by adapting word meanings on the basis of context, allowing them to generate contextually relevant responses and insights.
- LLMs offer transformative potential in analyzing and understanding conversations by representing text through embeddings, adapting meanings through transformers, and effectively processing the text.
- A significant cultural divide exists between engineers/scientists who develop AI systems and social researchers/humanists who study human behavior. The chapter advocates for an approach that combines technological expertise with a deep understanding of human discourse.
- The book presents detailed analyses of movie conversations to illustrate the complexities of conversations and the capabilities of LLMs, emphasizing the didactic value of such examples for understanding human interactions and AI technology.

NOTES

1 https://www.etymonline.com/word/conversation
2 https://ancientlanguages.org/latin/dictionary/verto-vertere-verti-versum#:~:text=vertere%20(Latin%20verb)%20%2D%20%22to%20turn%22%20%2D%20Allo%20Latin
3 https://en.wikipedia.org/wiki/Pulp_Fiction
4 https://openai.com/index/searchgpt-prototype/
5 https://www.youtube.com/playlist?list=PLZHQObOWTQDNU6R1_67000Dx_ZCJB-3pi
6 https://platform.openai.com/docs/concepts

REFERENCES

Bak, P. (2013). *How Nature Works: The Science of Self-organized Criticality.* New York, NY: Springer Science & Business Media.

Goffman, E. (1955). On face-work: An analysis of ritual elements in social interaction. *Psychiatry, 18*(3), 213–231.

Harries-Jones, P. (1995). *A Recursive Vision: Ecological Understanding and Gregory Bateson*. Toronto: University of Toronto Press.

Holquist, M. (1990). Dialogism. London: Routledge.

Kintsch, W. (1998). *Comprehension: A Paradigm for Cognition*. Cambridge: Cambridge University Press.

Neelakantan, A., Xu, T., Puri, R., et al. (2022). Text and code embeddings by contrastive pre-training. *arXiv preprint arXiv:2201.10005*.

Neuman, Y. (2013). Shakespeare's first sonnet: Reading through repetitions. *Semiotica*, 195, 119–126.

Neuman, Y. (2024). *AI for Understanding Context*. NY: Springer-Nature.

Neuman, Y., Bekerman, Z., & Kaplan, A. (2002). Rhetoric as the contextual manipulation of self and nonself. *Research on Language and Social Interaction*, 35(1), 93–112.

Neuman, Y., & Cohen, Y. (2024). A data set of synthetic utterances for computational personality analysis. *Scientific Data*, 11(1), 623.

Neuman, Y., Danesi, M., & Vilenchik, D. (2022). *Using AI for Dialoguing with Texts: From Psychology to Cinema and Literature*. London: Routledge.

Neuman, Y., & Levi, M. (2003). Blood and chocolate: A rhetorical approach to fear appeal. *Journal of Language and Social Psychology*, 22(1), 29–46.

Sznycer, D., & Lukaszewski, A. W. (2019). The emotion–valuation constellation: Multiple emotions are governed by a common grammar of social valuation. *Evolution and Human Behavior*, 40(4), 395–404.

2

AI FOR ANALYZING DIVERGENT PERSPECTIVES IN A CONVERSATION

PERSPECTIVES ARE IMPORTANT

One important aspect of understanding social interactions is the different perspectives of the interlocutors. Put simply, a *perspective* is how a participant *uniquely* represents the situation in which he is involved. Here is a simple example. Three colleagues decide to eat together. One is a vegetarian Buddhist, the second is an orthodox Jew, and the third is a Texan evangelist. The participants have different perspectives on what it is morally possible to eat. When they observe a buffet of food, different representations form in their minds. Unless we understand these perspectives and their divergence, we cannot understand the situation and the participants' behavior. Here is another example. In March 2021, the United States and China held a high-profile diplomatic meeting in Anchorage, Alaska.[1] This meeting marked the first significant in-person talks between the two countries since President Biden took office. The discussions were led by US Secretary of State Antony Blinken and National Security Advisor Jake Sullivan on the American side. The Chinese delegation was represented by Yang Jiechi, Director of the Office of the Central Commission for Foreign Affairs, and Foreign Minister Wang

DOI: 10.1201/9781003591047-2

Yi. The meeting was notable for its tense atmosphere, highlighting the deep-seated differences between the two global superpowers on various issues, including human rights, trade, cybersecurity, and China's actions in Hong Kong, Xinjiang, and the South China Sea. The opening statements I analyze in this chapter were marked by unusually blunt rhetoric, with both sides criticizing each other's policies and actions. Reading the opening statements from a pre-theoretical stance, that is, without clear theoretical guidelines, we can easily sense the tension and acknowledge the different perspectives of the participants. They simply see things differently. There is no need for expert analysis or sophisticated technologies to get a basic understanding of the meeting. However, getting a *deep* understanding of the different perspectives is not so trivial.

The opening comments are not the best example of what we call a conversation. However, they can be seen as a conversation, as each speaker responds to the others. In this context, one may ask whether large language models (LLMs) can help us to understand the conversation better. In this chapter, I would like to answer this question positively by showing how the model can enrich our representation of the conversation and give us a deeper and more detailed understanding of the participants' divergent perspectives.

Let me begin by presenting slices from Blinken's opening remarks. His utterance opens with greetings, which is a type of speech act:

> Well, good afternoon, and welcome. On behalf of national security adviser Sullivan and myself, I want to welcome Director Yang and State Councilor Wang to Alaska, and to thank you very much for making the journey to be with us.

Blinken continues by reporting that he returned

> [...] from meetings with Secretary of Defense [Lloyd] Austin and our counterparts in Japan and the Republic of Korea, two of our nation's closest allies who "were very interested in the discussions that we'll have here today and tomorrow because the issues that we'll raise are relevant not only to China and the United States, but to others across the region and indeed around the world.

In contrast with the opening speech act of greeting, it is unclear what Blinken is trying to achieve in his subsequent utterance. Why mention Japan and Korea?

Blinken continues by explaining:

> Our administration is committed to leading with diplomacy to advance the interests of the United States and to strengthen the rules-based international order... The alternative to a rules-based order is a world in which might make right and winners take all, and that would be a far more violent and unstable world for all of us.

It says that the United States is committed to a rules-based international order with only one alternative: violence that would result in an unstable world. Although nothing is explicitly said about the Chinese, it is implied that the Chinese alternative to the American one is violent and might destabilize the whole world.

Imagine you are an educated journalist addressing Blinken in a press conference with the following question:

> Secretary of State Antony Blinken, in your opening comment, you argued that the US is committed to a rules-based order and that the alternative is violence that would destabilize the world order. Are you suggesting that the Chinese promote a violent approach, destabilizing the world order?

I doubt whether Blinken's response would have answered your question in the affirmative. "I have never suggested anything like this," Blinken would probably have answered. The journalist may insist, saying, "But sir, this meaning is implied by your utterance." "Not at all," Blinken could have answered, "implied meaning is a matter of interpretation." In the following sections, I would like to remove the fog from this diplomatic discourse and show that LLMs supported by theory and scientific measures can take us beyond subjective interpretations. While utterances may be ambiguous and have several possible interpretations, some interpretations are better than others.

CONTEXT-ENRICHED EMBEDDINGS

My analysis focuses on the comments/utterances made by each participant. As explained before, the model represents the meaning of texts through embeddings. I used *OpenAI embeddings*[2] to represent each utterance as an embedding with a very high dimensionality. The dimensionality of OpenAI text-embedding-3-large is reflected in a vector with 3072 components. The embedding used by OpenAI is based on the model already trained to build the mind of the system.

The existence of a pretrained model limits LLMs. Therefore, an LLM might perform suboptimally when challenged with tasks requiring *updated knowledge* the model does not have and *domain-specific issues* requiring domain expertise. There are two general approaches to address these shortcomings. The first involves fine-tuning the general model to the specific task. The second is called *Retrieval Augmented Intelligence* (RAG).[3] RAG does not involve fine-tuning of the model but instead uses external data resources. In a later chapter dealing with personality analysis of the speakers in a conversation, I will use academic papers as external data resources. Both approaches have their pros and cons. Here, I adopt a different approach in which I enrich the context of the model by asking it to identify the dimensions of an utterance and adding them to the original embedding of the utterance. In other words, I 'frame' the representation of each utterance and add this frame to the embedding, or the representation, that OpenAI automatically generates. What I would like to explain through this move is *how to adapt the general mind of an LLM to a specific context* and avoid the need to fine-tune the whole model or to use external resources. The case presented and analyzed in this chapter only illustrates this general approach.

Using this approach, I enriched each utterance by including several 'frames.' By frames, I mean top-level *schemes* that may guide the analysis. I *prompt* the model to identify these frames. In the context of LLMs, a prompt refers to the input or query presented to the model to generate a response. It serves as a set of instructions, questions, or text that guides the model in producing relevant output. Depending on the desired outcome, the prompt can range from a simple question to more complex and detailed instructions like those I use in this book. You can consult Neuman (2024) to learn how to construct a good prompt.

The first frame I used was *ambiance*. Ambiance is the mood, character, quality, tone, atmosphere, etc., particularly of an environment or milieu. We already met this concept while discussing the conversation in Pulp Fiction. Why is it important to identify the ambiance expressed in the utterance? Because ambiance signals something general, holistic, and deep that we experience unconsciously. Exposing the ambiance expressed by an utterance, we can enrich our understanding of the conversation.

I used the prompt to identify the ambiance associated with each utterance. As a general guideline, I present each prompt with a numbered title and the word END, signaling the completion of the prompt. The words 'prompt' and 'end' are not included when prompting the model.

PROMPT 2.1

Ambiance is the mood, character, quality, tone, atmosphere, etc., particularly of an environment or milieu.
##
Describe the ambiance expressed in the following utterance:
[INSERT UTTERANCE HERE]
##
Output is in the form of seven points with one word for each point (e.g., SERENE, WARM).
##
END

For example, let us analyze an utterance to explain how the model identifies ambiance. The utterance is:

> I visited Tom yesterday. We sat in a wonderful coffee shop near his house and discussed the good old days when we were wild college students.

The model identified the following ambiance:

Nostalgic
Warm
Relaxed
Reflective
Comfortable
Pleasant
Familiar

To understand the meaning of an utterance, we can simply draw on the representation provided by OpenAI's embeddings. However, we can also extract some information, such as the ambiance, and add the outcome to the embedding of the original utterance. In several experiments I conducted with my engineer, I found that enriching the original utterance using the information provided by the model may significantly improve our understanding. So, the first step in enriching an utterance is to use the model to identify the ambiance, add the ambiance to the text of the original utterance, and form an updated embedding/representation of the utterance that includes both the original utterance and the ambiance.

The second frame that I used involved the *situation* reflected in the utterance. Situations concern the way subjects *represent* the context in which they operate. These representations may range from highly personal representations characterizing a given individual to highly objective representations shared by large collectives. I drew on my previous work to automatically measure the situational dimensions expressed in an utterance (Neuman & Cohen, 2023), using 100 statements representing situational dimensions. Here is the prompt I used to identify the situational dimension of an utterance:

PROMPT 2.2

Introduction:

> The Riverside Situational Q Sort (RSQ) is a method used in psychology to assess an individual's perception of their social environment. It involves sorting a set of statements or items based on how accurately they describe the individual's current situation or circumstances. The RSQ helps psychologists understand how people perceive and interpret their social context, which can provide insights into their thoughts, feelings, and behaviors in different situations.
>
> ##

Here are 100 statements corresponding with 100 situational dimensions:

> [LIST OF STATEMENTS HERE]
>
> ##

Instructions:

> Analyze the following utterance: [UTTERANCE HERE]
>
> ##
>
> Identify the seven statements that best represent the utterance.
>
> ##
>
> Output: The seven statements that best represent the utterance.
> END

Let me show you how nicely this prompt works in identifying situational dimensions. I return to the opening slice of conversation from Pulp Fiction that I presented previously and analyze the exchange between the young woman called by the man "Honey Bunny" and the young man called by his spouse "Pumpkin." The model identified the following situational dimensions:

1. It is a situation where someone tries to convince someone of something.
2. It is a situation where someone needs or desires reassurance.

3. It is a frustrating situation.
4. It is a situation that could make people tense and upset.
5. It is a situation that could arouse negative emotions.
6. It is a situation where people compare themselves to each other.
7. It is a situation where someone is being pressured to conform to the actions of others.

We see how good the model's output is as it corresponds with my previous analysis. At this point, we can revise the already revised embedding by adding the situational dimensions produced by the model.

The ambiance and the situational dimensions enrich the embedding of the utterance by adding high-level information. Previously, I mentioned the importance of a top-down approach. Here, I use this approach by enriching the representation of each utterance with top-down information that frames our understanding. Next, I add two additional sources of enrichment involving microlevel information: speech acts and content. These are not general frames but more specific aspects of the utterance. Speech acts were discussed earlier as an important construct for understanding a situation. Here is the prompt I used to identify the speech acts.

PROMPT 2.3

Instructions:
   Identify the speech acts in the utterance: [UTTERANCE HERE].
   ##
   Output: The list of speech acts in the utterance (e.g., greeting, criticizing, etc.).
   END

I now use the model's output and add the list of speech acts used in the utterance to the already revised embedding.

The last source I use involves several content categories important for understanding diplomatic discourse. We see them in the following prompt, where they are presented through theoretical and operational definitions.

A theoretical definition explains the idea in theoretical terms. For example, one of the dimensions I would like to identify in the utterance is the *key issue*. A theoretical definition of a key issue is:

> The main topic or problem central to a discussion, debate, or analysis.

In contrast with a theoretical definition, an operational definition presents the way we *measure* our dimension. The operational definition of a key issue may be as follows:

> Key issues are identified by listing the main topics or problems explicitly mentioned in a participant's speech or text.

Why is it important to present both types of definitions in the prompt? An important thing one needs to understand while working with LLMs is that a simple, clear, and detailed prompt is crucial if the model is to perform well. Like humans, the model needs to understand exactly what you are asking it to do. Here is the prompt:

PROMPT 2.4

> Here are nine dimensions that I would like you to identify in an utterance. Each dimension is labeled (e.g., 'key issues') and followed by theoretical and operational definitions of the dimension.
> ##
> The nine dimensions are:
>
> 1. Key issues
>   Theoretical definition: Key issues are the main topics or problems central to a discussion, debate, or analysis.
>
>   Operational definition: Key issues are identified by listing the main topics or problems mentioned explicitly in a participant's speech or text.

2. Stance

   Theoretical definition: The stance refers to a person's position or attitude regarding a particular issue or topic.

   Operational definition: The stance is determined by analyzing statements in a participant's speech or text that indicate support, opposition, neutrality, or alternative viewpoints on specific issues.

3. Values

   Theoretical definition: Values are the fundamental beliefs or standards that guide behavior and decision-making.

   Operational definition: Values are inferred from statements in a participant's speech or text emphasizing importance, worth, or priorities, such as references to fairness, justice, freedom, etc.

4. Principles

   Theoretical definition: Principles are fundamental truths or propositions that serve as the foundation for a system of belief or behavior.

   Operational definition: Principles are identified in a participant's speech or text by locating statements that refer to core beliefs or rules guiding actions, such as adherence to international law, human rights, etc.

5. Priorities

   Theoretical definition: Priorities are the preferences or areas of importance that a person or organization focuses on above all others.

   Operational definition: Priorities are determined by repeatedly noting the issues or goals a participant emphasizes or states as being most important in their speech or text.

6. Tone

   Theoretical definition: The tone is the attitude or emotional quality a speaker or writer conveys through their choice of words and style.

Operational definition: The tone is analyzed by examining the language, sentence structure, and overall style in a participant's speech or text to categorize it as formal, informal, serious, humorous, etc.

7. Approach
Theoretical definition: The approach refers to the method or strategy used to address a situation, issue, or problem.

Operational definition: The approach is identified by reviewing the specific actions or strategies a participant proposes or uses, as described in their speech or text, such as collaborative, confrontational, diplomatic, etc.

8. Historical and contextual references
Theoretical definition: Historical and contextual references mention past events, situations, or relevant background information that provide context to the current discussion.

Operational definition: Historical and contextual references are noted by identifying specific mentions of past events, historical context, or background information in a participant's speech or text.

9. Goals and objectives
Theoretical definition: Goals and objectives are the desired outcomes or targets that a person or organization aims to achieve.

Operational definition: Goals and objectives are determined by identifying explicit statements in a participant's speech or text that outline intended outcomes or targets, such as achieving peace, promoting economic growth, etc.

##

Instructions:
Identify the nine abovementioned dimensions in the following utterance: [UTTERANCE HERE]
END

The outcome of this prompt was additional information used to revise and enrich our original embedding.

The conversation is comprised of utterances generated by the participants: Secretary of State Antony Blinken, National Security Adviser Jake Sullivan, Chinese Director of the Office of the Central Commission for Foreign Affairs Yang Jiechi, and Foreign Minister Wang Yi. The sequence of speakers was:

Blinken, Sullivan, Yang, Wang, Blinken, Sullivan, Yang, Wang.

I symbolized the utterance generated by a speaker with a letter indicating the speaker's name and a number indicating the position of his utterance. The sequence of utterances is therefore symbolized as follows:

B1, S1, Y1, W1, B2, S2, Y2, W2

I used the model to enrich each utterance with information. This means that I used the model to extract more information from the utterance, added or 'glued' the information to the end of the utterance, and generated a revised embedding of the new text.

MEASURING DIVERGENCE

Now that we have an enriched embedding to represent the meaning of the utterance, the next task is to measure how much these representations diverge from each other. More specifically, I assume that each utterance represents the speaker's perspective. I measure the divergence of one perspective from the other by measuring the divergence between the enriched embedding of an utterance generated by the Chinese/American speaker and the enriched embedding of the utterances previously generated by each speaker of the other party. I thus analyze two utterances in each step, and the divergence is always measured between the

TABLE 2.1 The Measured Divergences

DIVERGENCE NUMBER	V_2	V_1
1	Y1	B1
2	Y1	S1
3	W1	B1
4	W1	S1
5	B2	Y1
6	B2	W1
7	S2	Y1
8	S2	W1
9	Y2	B2
10	Y2	S2
11	W2	B2
12	W2	S2

second (v_2) and the first utterance (v_1). Table 2.1 presents the list of divergences that I measured. For example, the first divergence is between the enriched embedding of the first utterance generated by Yang (Y1) and the enriched embedding of the first utterance previously generated by Blinken (B1).

In sum, the general strategy is to represent the two utterances through the enriched embedding and then measure the divergence of one embedding from the other.

Given two utterances, I first used OpenAI's embedding to generate embeddings for each utterance. I use the notations v_1 and v_2 to describe the embeddings, or vectors, corresponding to the two utterances. Each vector is a fixed array with 3072 dimensions. Therefore, the components are v_{1i} and v_{2i}, respectively, for $i = 1$, 2, …, 3072. For example, measuring how different Yang's first utterance is from the previous utterance generated by Blinken, I represented each utterance as an enriched array of numbers, a vector, with 3072 dimensions, where each dimension is represented by a number.

TABLE 2.2 Embeddings of 'Cat' and 'Rat'

CAT	RAT
0.2	0.3
0.1	0.0001
0.7	0.2
0.000001	0.5

To assess the divergence between the two utterances, I first calculate the *difference* between the two embeddings. This procedure involves calculating the differences between the corresponding components of the two vectors. Let me illustrate this step using a simple example. Assume you would like to identify the difference between the meanings of 'cat' and 'rat.' The embedding dimension is of length four, and the two corresponding embeddings are shown in Table 2.2.

Let **d** represent the difference between the two vectors:

$$\mathbf{d} = v_1 - v_2$$

This is the vector of differences. In the above example, this vector has components (0.2−0.3), (0.1−0.0001), and so on. To analyze the embeddings for the diplomatic discourse, I multiply each component of **d** by 100 to transform it into an integer and raise it to the power of 2 to emphasize the differences. Finally, I multiply each squared difference component by the corresponding component of the original vectors v_1 and v_2. The outcome of this procedure is two revised embeddings (i.e., vectors) *weighted* by emphasizing the differences between the enriched embeddings. In the next step, I computed the divergence between the embedding of utterance 2 (v_2) and the embedding of utterance 1 (v_1) using a new measure called the vector projection divergence.

THE VECTOR PROJECTION DIVERGENCE

I have devised a new measure called the vector projection divergence (VPD) to measure the divergence of perspectives. The VPD is analogous to the Kullback-Leibler divergence, but with respect to vectors. As this measure involves some mathematical technicalities, I will explain it step by step, using an example from *The Simpsons*. You may skip this section if mathematics repulses you. However, I would invite you to bear with me, as my explanation is self-contained, user-friendly, and requires minimal calculations.

The Simpsons was an iconic animated TV series featuring Homer, Marge Simpson, and their children. You will recall Homer and Marge's different personas if you have watched the series. If you are unfamiliar with it, suffice it to say that they are quite different. Here, I would like to show how Homer and Marge may see each other differently; in other words, to show how their *perspectives* of each other diverge. To address this challenge, I provided the model with the following prompt:

PROMPT 2.5

Imagine that you are Homer Simpson.
Homer, please describe your wife, Marge, using five adjectives.
    Use the adjectives that immediately come to your mind.
END

The model describes Marge as follows: loyal, patient, caring, smart, loving, and beautiful.

Repeating the same instruction for Marge, the model describes Homer as, goofy, clumsy, big-hearted, and lazy. Next, I merged the lists of adjectives and asked the model to perform *semantic clustering*. The model identified the following semantic clusters:

Cluster 1: Affectionate and caring

Loyal
Caring
Loving
Patient
Big-hearted

Cluster 2: Intellectual and appearance

Smart
Beautiful

Cluster 3: Behavioral traits

Goofy
Clumsy
Lazy

Let us now map the adjectives used by Homer and Marge to these clusters. The first cluster is 'affectionate and caring.' It includes four adjectives used by Homer to describe Marge (e.g., loyal and caring) and one adjective used by Marge to describe Homer (i.e., loving and big-hearted). We see that Homer's representation of Marge in terms of affection and caring is much stronger than Marge's representation of Homer in terms of affection and caring. I performed that same counting analysis for all the clusters and generated the following array of numbers (i.e., vectors) for Homer's description of Marge and Marge's description of Homer (Table 2.3).

This 3-dimensional embedding represents how each character perceives the other. Therefore, it is a simple embedding representing the perspective of each character.

In my proposed analysis, each perspective is represented as a vector. I start with two vectors, v_1 and v_2. The decision of which vector is v_1 and which vector is v_2 is arbitrary, but I always measure the divergence of v_2 from v_1. Let me start by measuring the divergence of Marge's perspective of Homer (v_2) from Homer's perspective of Marge (v_1).

To compute the divergence of v_2 from v_1, I first compute the projection of v_2 onto v_1. The projection is calculated as follows:

Projection of v_2 onto v_1:

$$\text{Proj}v_1\mathbf{v}_2 = \frac{v_2 \cdot v_1}{v_1 \cdot v_1} v_1$$

TABLE 2.3 The Perspectives of Homer and Marge

HOMER DESCRIBING MARGE	MARGE DESCRIBING HOMER
4	1
2	0
0	3

where $v_2 \cdot v_1$ is the scalar product of the two vectors. The scalar product of two vectors, or the dot product, is a mathematical operation that takes two vectors and returns a single scalar (a number). Let me illustrate this operation with respect to the vectors for Homer and Marge. The scalar product of these vectors is

$$v_1 \cdot v_2 = (4 \times 1) + (2 \times 0) + (0 \times 3) = 4$$

The scalar product $v_1 \cdot v_1$ is

$$(4 \times 4) + (2 \times 2) + (0 \times 0) = 20$$

Dividing 4 by 20, we get 0.2, and we perform the multiplication

$$0.2 \times [4,\ 2,\ 0]$$

to get

$$[0.8,\ 0.4,\ 0]$$

What is the meaning of this projection? The projection of v_2 onto v_1 represents the component of v_2 that is in the same direction as v_1.

Next, I compute the *projection error*. What is the meaning of this error? This is the part of v_2 not captured by v_1:

$$\text{Errorv}_1(\mathbf{v_2}) = \mathbf{v_2} - \text{Projv}_1\mathbf{v_2}$$

The projection error is the difference between the original vector v_2 and its projection onto v_1. It represents the part of v_2 that is not captured by the projection, showing how much v_2 deviates from being in the direction of v_1. Applying it to the Simpsons, I get

$$[1,\ 0,\ 3] - [0.8,\ 0.4,\ 0] = [0.2,\ -0.4,\ 3]$$

Finally, I compute the divergence measure as the magnitude of this vector:

$$\text{Dv}_1(\mathbf{v_2}) = \left\| \mathbf{v_2} - \text{Projv}_1\mathbf{v_2} \right\| = \left\| \mathbf{v_2} - \frac{v_2 \cdot v_1}{v_1 \cdot v_1} v_1 \right\|$$

This measure represents how much the embedding v_2 is not aligned with the embedding v_1 or how much the embedding v_2 diverges from being a scaled version of the embedding v_1. It is the magnitude (length) of the projection error vector and quantifies how different v_2 is from v_1.

This measure is clearly non-negative, and it is important to realize that it is asymmetric: for example, the divergence of Yang's utterance from Blinken's utterance is probably not the same as the divergence of Blinken's from Yang's.

In the case of the Simpsons, the divergence score is the norm (magnitude) of the projection error:

$$\sqrt{0.2^2 + -0.4^2 + 3^2} = 3.03$$

Therefore, the final divergence score is 3.03.

This score measures the extent to which Marge's perspective of Homer diverges from Homer's perspective of Marge. But what happens if we switch the vectors and measure the divergence between Homer's perspective of Marge and Marge's perspective of Homer? In this case, the score is higher: 4.29. Understanding this asymmetry of perspectives is perhaps a little challenging, but it can be explained as follows.

In plain terms, the asymmetry between Marge's and Homer's perspectives means that they don't see each other in exactly the same way. Homer has a broader, more varied view of Marge than she has of him. This difference shows up in the numbers: Homer's view of Marge diverges more from the way Marge sees Homer (with a divergence score of 4.29) than how Marge's view diverges from Homer's (with a score of 3.03). Marge's lower divergence score (3.03) may indicate that her view of Homer is somewhat more aligned with Homer's view of her, suggesting that Marge might have a more consistent or stable perception of Homer, with fewer discrepancies between her view and his. This interpretation is in line with the personality of the two characters, as Marge is the more mature and stable figure in the family. This suggests that Marge might not expect as much from Homer in terms of fulfilling various roles. She might focus more on the practical side of their relationship, not only appreciating his good heart but also recognizing his flaws. This can lead to a better grounded and more realistic view of their relationship. Moreover, the divergence scores might also reflect the roles that Homer and Marge believe they play in their relationship. The higher divergence in Homer's view could suggest that he sees Marge as playing a more significant or varied role in their life together, while Marge's simpler view of Homer might indicate she sees him more in terms of a few key traits.

Let me sum up the procedure for computing the divergence of one utterance from the other. Given two utterances, the vector of utterance 1 is v_1, and the vector of utterance 2 is v_2. The process of measuring the divergence of utterance 2 from utterance 1 can be summarized as follows:[4]

1. Compute the dot product of v_2 and v_1
2. Compute the dot product of v_1 and v_1
3. Find the ratio between the first and the second result
4. Multiply the value you produced in step 3 by v_1
5. Find the difference between v_2 and the vector produced in step 4
6. Find the length (magnitude) of the vector produced in step 5

DIVERGING PERSPECTIVES IN THE ALASKA MEETING

So far, I have focused on rather technical methodological issues. I showed how to enrich the representation of the original utterance using the LLM and how to measure the divergence between two utterances. Here, I would like to show how the results of this procedure may empower our understanding of the meeting. Using VPD, I computed the divergence between the utterances. Table 2.4 presents the results of the six highest divergence scores.[5]

The divergence scores show that in five out of six cases (~83%), the divergence is between a *Chinese speaker* and an *American speaker*.

TABLE 2.4 The Top Six Divergence Scores of the Participants in the Diplomatic Meeting

DIVERGENCE	SCORE
W2 from S2	2.89
W2 from B2	1.8
Y1 from S1	1.47
S2 from W1	0.97
Y1 from B1	0.54
Y2 from B2	0.03

These results expose a strong asymmetry in the divergence of the speakers' perspectives. The Chinese perspectives diverge much more from those of the Americans. Figure 2.1 visualizes this pattern. An arrow indicates the divergence of one utterance/perspective from the other.

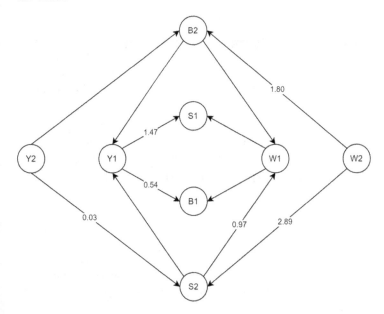

FIGURE 2.1 Visualizing the top divergence scores.

We can see that Yang's first utterance diverges from both Blinken's and Sullivan's in the first round and that Wang's utterance diverges from both Blinken's and Sullivan's in the second round. This high-level analysis shows the asymmetric divergence between the parties' perspectives.

Is there a simple way to explain this divergence? From a bird's eye view, an immediate conclusion is that more effort would be required to align the American perspective with the Chinese than vice versa. This is an important finding. Based on the following detailed analysis, it can be explained as follows. Both the Chinese and the Americans praise their own achievements. Still, despite the similarities, the American perspective is blind to the Chinese anger resulting from their feeling of being devalued and disrespected by the Americans. In the next section, I will dig deeper into the analysis and explain the source of the Chinese divergence.

EXPLAINING THE DIVERGENCE

First, I tried to explain the divergence in terms of ambiance. To measure the ambiance in an utterance, I used the following input:

Input: Utterance 1 and utterance 2.
    Utterance 1: [UTTERANCE 1 HERE]
    Utterance 2: [UTTERANCE 2 HERE]

And the following prompt:

PROMPT 2.6

Ambiance is the mood, character, quality, tone, atmosphere, etc., particularly of an environment or milieu.
##

Describe the ambiance expressed in EACH UTTERANCE.
##

Output is in the form of seven points with one word for each point (e.g., SERENE, WARM).
##

Merge the two lists of words into a single list of 14 words.
**

Use the following prompt:
Perform semantic clustering on the merged list of ambiance words.

Output: A list of semantic clusters.
**

For Utterance 1 and Utterance 2
Count the number of ambiance words in each semantic category for each utterance.
##

Create vectors:
List the semantic clusters in a consistent order.
For each semantic cluster, record the count from Utterance 1 and Utterance 2 as components of a vector.
Output Format:
Present the counts as vectors, with each component corresponding to the count of a semantic cluster in the order listed.

END

For example, the first statements of Blinken and Wang produced a merged list of the following ambiance words:

1. Diplomatic
2. Formal
3. Concerned
4. Assertive
5. Direct
6. Cautious

7. Professional
8. Defensive
9. Resentful
10. Firm
11. Critical
12. Nationalistic
13. Determined
14. Hopeful

And with the following semantic clusters:

1. **Diplomatic**: Diplomatic, Formal, Professional
2. **Tense**: Concerned, Cautious, Defensive, Resentful, Critical
3. **Assertive**: Assertive, Direct, Firm, Determined
4. **Positive**: Hopeful

Translated into the following count:

Utterance 1 (Blinken):
   Diplomatic: 3
   Tense: 2
   Assertive: 2
   Positive: 0
   Utterance 2 (Wang):
   Diplomatic: 0
   Tense: 5
   Assertive: 2
   Positive: 1

And the following vectors:

$v_1 = [3, 2, 2, 0]$
$v_2 = [0, 5, 2, 1]$

We can see a difference in the way each interlocutor's opening utterance created the atmosphere. The representation of ambiance

TABLE 2.5 The Divergence of Ambiance

DIVERGENCE	VPD
Y1 divergence from B1	4.30
Y1 divergence from S1	3.90
W1 divergence from B1	4.30
W1 divergence from S1	4.26
B2 divergence from Y1	4.83
B2 divergence from W1	4.30
S2 divergence from Y1	4.50
S2 divergence from W1	4.36
Y2 divergence from S2	5.00
Y2 divergence from B2	4.30
W2 divergence from B2	4.30
W2 divergence from S2	5.80

represents each participant's perspective on the conversation. We can see that Blinken is far more diplomatic, and Wang is far more tense. The divergence is expressed, for instance, through the greater efforts required by Blinken to understand the tense atmosphere. Whenever greater efforts are required, we can infer the existence of a blind spot.

Next, I use the VPD to measure the divergence in ambiance for all participants. In other words, I measured the divergence between the ambiance expressed in utterance 2 and that expressed in utterance 1.

The ambiance divergence scores are presented in Table 2.5, followed by a graphical representation where the highest scores are marked on the arrows.

We can see that the highest divergence in ambiance is between Wang's concluding utterance and Sullivan's previous utterance (Figure 2.2).

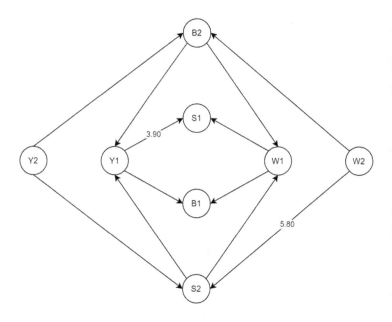

FIGURE 2.2 Visualizing the divergence of ambiance.

Analyzing the ambiance expressed by these utterances, we find the following:

Ambiance Words for Each Utterance

Utterance 1 (Sullivan):
1. Confident
2. Collaborative
3. Progressive
4. Inspiring
5. Open
6. Hopeful
7. Dignified

Utterance 2 (Wang):

1. Questioning
2. Defensive
3. Skeptical
4. Critical
5. Cautious
6. Respectful
7. Direct

Semantic Clustering of Ambiance Words:

1. **Positive assertiveness**

   Confident

   Progressive

   Inspiring

   Hopeful

2. **Collaboration and respect**

   Collaborative

   Open

   Respectful

   Dignified

3. **Questioning and critique**

   Questioning

   Skeptical

   Critical

4. **Defensiveness and caution**

   Defensive

   Cautious

   Direct

Resulting vectors for the utterances

$\mathbf{v}_1$: $[4, 3, 0, 0]$
$\mathbf{v}_2$: $[0, 2, 3, 2]$

Now we can better understand the divergence between Wang's utterance and Sullivan's utterance. The divergence seems to be grounded in Wang's *critical* and *defensive* ambiance. Similarly to the previous analysis, the American blind spot is expressed through their inability to appreciate the tense, critical, and defensive Chinese stance. To better understand the divergence, we turn to the analysis of the situational dimensions. I used the following prompt:

PROMPT 2.7

Introduction:

The RSQ is a method used in psychology to assess an individual's perception of their social environment. It involves sorting a set of statements or items based on how accurately they describe the individual's current situation or circumstances. The RSQ helps psychologists understand how people perceive and interpret their social context, which can provide insights into their thoughts, feelings, and behaviors in different situations.

##

Here are the 100 statements corresponding with 100 situational dimensions:

[A DESCRIPTION OF THE 100 SITUATIONS HERE]

##

Instructions

Input

Utterance 1: [UTTERANCE 1 HERE]

Utterance 2: [UTTERANCE 2 HERE]

##

For each text:

Use the 100 statements to analyze the text.

Identify the 12 statements that best represent the text.

##

For each identified and unique statement, count the number of times it appears in Utterance 1 and utterance 2.

##

Create vectors:

    List the identified statements in a consistent order.

    For each statement, record the count from utterance 1 and utterance 2 as elements of a vector.

    ##

Output Format:

    Present the counts as vectors, with each element corresponding to the count of a statement in the order listed.

    END

With respect to the situations, I found that in seven out of twelve cases ($\sim$58%), the divergence was 0. In most cases, both sides see the situation in the same way. In the other cases, the divergence is the same (VPD $= 1.36$) except for *one noticeable case* where the divergence of Y2 from S2 is 2.54. This is an interesting finding, as the divergence between the Chinese correspondent's utterance and Sullivan's second utterance already appeared when considering the ambiance. It seems that Sullivan's second comment resulted in a significant gap, not only in terms of ambiance but also in terms of how the Chinese conceived the situation. The situations that have been identified with respect to Y2 and S2 are:

1. The situation involves someone who is trying to impress
2. The situation involves someone who is trying to convince someone of something
3. The situation involves a job that needs to be done
4. It is a situation where talking is expected or demanded
5. The situation is potentially enjoyable
6. The situation is playful
7. The situation involves someone who needs help
8. The situation involves someone who is criticizing
9. The situation involves someone unhappy or suffering
10. The situation involves someone trying to dominate or boss others
11. The situation involves someone who is blaming another for something

12. The situation involves someone trying to control others rather than permit them to control him/her
13. The situation involves someone trying to get his/her way regardless of what others in the group may want

The two corresponding vectors are:

v_1: $[1, 1, 1, 1, 1, 1, 1, 0, 0, 0, 0, 0, 0]$
v_2: $[0, 1, 0, 0, 0, 0, 0, 1, 1, 1, 1, 1, 1]$

Clustering the situations, I identified six semantic clusters of situations. One cluster is titled 'Domination and control,' and it includes the following situations:

1. The situation involves someone trying to dominate or boss others
2. The situation involves someone who is blaming another for something
3. The situation involves someone trying to control others rather than permit them to control him/her
4. The situation involves someone trying to get his/her way regardless of what others in the group may want

The vectors for the semantic clusters of the situations are:

v_1: $[2, 2, 2, 1, 0, 0]$
v_2: $[1, 0, 0, 0, 2, 4]$

Comparing the vectors, I found that utterance Y2 is less involved in a task-oriented situation (e.g., the situation involves a job that needs to be done) or in a playful situation but significantly more in control and criticism. This means Yang's second comment diverges from Sullivan's previous comment in that it represents a negatively charged situation that Sullivan's task-oriented and playful representation cannot easily comprehend. The elephant in Alaska's meeting room is not the tension explicitly identified by the commentators and journalists but the *asymmetry of perspectives*, expressing a clear imbalance in the way the two sides conceive the situation. We repeatedly find that the Americans have a blind spot with respect to the negative emotions experienced by the Chinese side.

Can we improve our understanding by analyzing the divergence of the speech acts? I used the following prompt and analyzed the divergence regarding the speech acts.

PROMPT 2.8

Instructions:

Input: Utterance 1 and utterance 2.

Utterance 1: [UTTERANCE 1 HERE]

Utterance 2: [UTTERANCE 2 HERE]

##

Identify the Speech Acts:

Read through utterance 1 and utterance 2.

For each utterance, identify the different speech acts being used.

##

Merge the list of speech acts into an integrated list of speech acts.

##

For each identified speech act in the integrated list, count the number of times it appears in utterance 1 and utterance 2.

##

Create Vectors:

List the identified speech acts in a consistent order.

For each speech act, record the count from utterance 1 and utterance 2 as elements of a vector.

##

Output Format:

Present the counts as vectors, with each element corresponding to the count of a speech act in the order listed.

##

Example:

Assume the identified speech acts are:

Greeting and Welcoming

Informing/Reporting

Stating Purpose/Commitment

Warning/Cautioning

Proposing/Planning

Expressing Concerns

Clarifying/Explaining

Predicting/Anticipating

Stating Intent

Thanking/Appreciating

Requesting

Addressing/Acknowledging

Denying/Rejecting

Accusing/Blaming

Asserting/Declaring

Referencing/Reminding

Emphasizing/Highlighting

Closing

You will then have:

A vector for utterance 1: [count1, count2, count3, ..., count18]

A vector for utterance 2: [count1, count2, count3, ..., count18]

Where count1 is the count of "Greeting and Welcoming" in utterance 1, count2 is the count of "Informing/Reporting" in utterance 1, and so on. Similarly, count1 for Utterance 2 corresponds to the count of "Greeting and Welcoming" in utterance 2, count2 for utterance 2 corresponds to the count of "Informing/Reporting" in utterance 2, and so on.

END

The following speech acts were identified in the utterances of Sullivan and Wang:

1. Greeting and Welcoming
2. Informing/Reporting
3. Stating Purpose/Commitment
4. Clarifying/Explaining
5. Thanking/Appreciating
6. Expressing Concerns
7. Accusing/Blaming
8. Asserting/Declaring
9. Referencing/Reminding
10. Emphasizing/Highlighting
11. Closing

The corresponding vectors are:

$\mathbf{v}_1$: $[2, 4, 2, 3, 1, 0, 0, 0, 0, 0, 0]$
$\mathbf{v}_2$: $[0, 0, 0, 0, 0, 3, 2, 4, 2, 2, 2]$

Two clear points of divergence occur with respect to the category of informing/reporting, where Sullivan says:

1. "A confident country is able to look hard at its own shortcomings and constantly seek to improve."
2. "The other secret sauce of America is that our people are a problem-solving people."
3. "Just a couple of weeks ago, the United States landed another rover on Mars, and it wasn't just an American project."
4. "It had technology from multiple countries from Europe and other parts of the world."

The speech acts used in this category are statements expressing self-praise and superiority. In contrast, Yang's major category of speech acts is 'Asserting/Declaring,' where the most dominant statement is:

> So let me say here that, in front of the Chinese side, the United States does not have the qualification to say that it wants to speak to China from a position of strength.

We see that the repeated divergence from Sullivan's second utterance indicates the divergence we identified on the higher level of analysis. Sullivan's representation of the American side presents an assertive approach and superiority. Although Wang does not directly respond to Sullivan, his concluding comment is in a different spirit:

> But if the United States is interested in having those discussions with China, then we are ready to have those discussions with the US side, but based on **mutual respect** so that we can increase our **mutual understanding** on those issues (my emphasis).

The speech acts used by Sullivan emphasized self-praise and were conceived by the Chinese as an attempt to speak with China on non-equal terms. Indeed, the situation reflected in Sullivan's utterance involves impression management. Sullivan's stance might have been conceived in the following way by the Chinese side: We Americans are great; those who work with us benefit, so let's have some fun. The situation, as reflected in Yang's utterance, is different. His opening comment is:

> Well, it was my bad. When I entered this room, I should have reminded the U.S. side of paying attention to its tone in our respective opening remarks, but I didn't.

Yang criticizes the American side for trying to patronize China and hold the conversation from a position of strength. His stance is that of an individual experiencing disrespect. The anger expressed in this utterance can be explained through the theory of emotions as a response to conceived devaluation. Although the Chinese representatives also praise themselves, the American side does not conceive it as a patronizing and disrespectful approach. This gap between the Chinese and the Americans is asymmetric; the two sides don't understand their similarities and differences.

FROM DIVERGENCE TO SIMILARITIES AND DIFFERENCES

Previously, I focused on explaining the divergence between Wang and Sullivan. I now take the model further by asking it to identify *similarities* and *differences* between the content categories expressed by the utterances. First, I prompted the model to identify the content:

PROMPT 2.9

Here are nine dimensions that I would like you to identify in an utterance. Each dimension is labeled (e.g., 'key issues') and followed by theoretical and operational definitions of the dimension.
##
The nine dimensions:
[DESCRIPTION OF THE NINE DIMENSIONS HERE]
##
Instructions:
Identify the nine abovementioned dimensions in each of the following texts:
Utterance 1: [Utterance 1 HERE]
Utterance 2: [Utterance 2 HERE]
##
END

In the next step, I asked the model to identify *similarities* and *differences* between the two utterances:

PROMPT 2.10

Identify the SIMILARITIES between the dimensions expressed in each utterance.
Output: A list of similarities. Label the list as 'Similarity.'

##
Identify the DIFFERENCES between the dimensions expressed in
each utterance.
Output: A list of differences. Label the list as 'Difference.'
##
END

The next step was to measure the divergence between each utterance and its *differences* and *similarities* with the previous utterance (i.e.,
utterance 1). This move is slightly more complicated but illustrates
how far we can take LLMs. To address this challenge, I formed
embeddings for the following pieces of text:

1. Utterance 2
2. the differences between the two utterances, and
3. the similarities between the two utterances

The procedure was as follows:

For utterance 2 and utterance 1 (e.g., Y1 and B1).
Use the LLM and the prompt I gave to extract the nine categories
from each utterance and their SIMILARITIES and DIFFERENCES.
Compute the embedding of SIMILARITIES (EmbedSIM) and
DIFFERENCES (EmbedDIFF).
Compute the embedding of utterance 2 (EmbedText2)
Use the VPD and compute the divergence of EmbedText2 from
(1) EmbedSIM and (2) EmbedDIFF

Let me explain the procedure in simple terms. The model identifies similarities and differences between the content categories
expressed by the utterances. Next, I embed or represent the second
utterance, the similarities, and the differences. Finally, I use the VPD
to measure *the divergence of the utterance from its (1) similarities and (2) differences with the previous utterance.* This procedure allows us to quantify the
extent to which a perspective diverges from its similarities and differences with the other perspective.

Using this procedure, I found that the highest divergence concerning differences was for the divergence of utterance Y2 from utterance S2. We have already learned that the Chinese conceived of Sullivan as representing a patronizing and disrespectful stance. To further explain the Chinese divergence from Sullivan, let me delve deeper into the analysis of Sullivan's second utterance (S2) and Yang's response (Y2).

The nine dimensions produced for each utterance appear below. They teach us that Sullivan presents a confident approach with a call for collaboration. However, the utterance by Yang shows that a key issue for the Chinese is the American 'tone' and their respect for China, or lack of it. Here is the content analysis of the utterances.

FOR S2

Key Issues

"A confident country is able to look hard at its own shortcomings and constantly seek to improve."

"We believe we solve problems best when we work together with allies and partners around the world."

"The United States landed another rover on Mars, and it wasn't just an American project."

"It had technology from multiple countries from Europe and other parts of the world."

"The opportunity for us to explain where we're coming from, to hear where you are coming from and to indicate, at bottom, what our principles, our priorities and our long-term strategies are."

Stance

Support for international collaboration: "We believe we solve problems best when we work together with allies and partners around the world."

Support for innovation and improvement: "A confident country is able to look hard at its own shortcomings and constantly seek to improve."

Values

"Human dignity and human rights that are truly universal."
"Constantly seeking to produce the kind of progress that benefits all of us."

Principles

Collaboration: "working closely with others."
Reinvention and improvement: "a country that is constantly reinventing itself."

Priorities

International collaboration: "working together with allies and partners around the world."
Progress and innovation: "constantly seeking to produce the kind of progress that benefits all of us."

Tone

Confident: "a confident country."
Hopeful: "constantly seeking to produce the kind of progress that benefits all of us."
Collaborative: "working together with allies and partners around the world."

Approach

Collaborative: "working closely with others."
Open and inclusive: "the opportunity for us to explain where we're coming from, to hear where you are coming from."

Historical and Contextual References

"Just a couple of weeks ago, the United States landed another rover on Mars."

Goals and Objectives

Promote international collaboration and progress: "constantly seeking to produce the kind of progress that benefits all of us."

Engage in open dialogue: "the opportunity for us to explain where we're coming from, to hear where you are coming from."

FOR Y2

In contrast, the content analysis for Y2 resulted in the following outcome.

Key Issues

"The tone of the U.S. side."

"In a condescending way from a position of strength."

"Necessary diplomatic protocols."

"Cooperation benefits both sides."

"The expectation of the people of the world."

Stance

Opposition to condescension: "The United States does not have the qualification to say that it wants to speak to China from a position of strength."

Support for cooperation: "Cooperation benefits both sides."

Values

Respect: "necessary diplomatic protocols."

Cooperation: "cooperation benefits both sides."

Principles

Equality in dialogue: "The United States does not have the qualification to say that it wants to speak to China from a position of strength."

Respect for diplomatic protocols: "necessary diplomatic protocols."

Priorities

Respectful dialogue: "necessary diplomatic protocols."
Emphasizing cooperation: "cooperation benefits both sides."

Tone

Defensive: "The Chinese side felt compelled to make this speech because of the tone of the US side."
Accusatory: "Isn't this the intention of the United States?"
Emphasizing equality: "The United States does not have the qualification to say that it wants to speak to China from a position of strength."

Approach

Confrontational: "The United States does not have the qualification to say that it wants to speak to China from a position of strength."
Emphasizing protocol: "necessary diplomatic protocols."

Historical and Contextual References

"Even 20 years or 30 years back."
"China started being encircled by foreign countries."

Goals and Objectives

Ensure respectful and equal dialogue: "necessary diplomatic protocols."
Emphasize the importance of cooperation: "Cooperation benefits both sides."

It is clear that the content categories differ, but too much information may hinder our analysis. Instead of overloading our minds with comparisons, I can simply ask the model to identify the *differences* between the two utterances. Here is the comparison the model generated.

Key Issues

Utterance 1 focuses on international collaboration, progress, and innovation.

Utterance 2 focuses on addressing the tone of the US side and the need for respectful dialogue.

We see that the first difference is between abstract key issues and the conceived tone of the Americans. It is not surprising, therefore, that with respect to stance, Yang's utterance is defensive and critical:

Stance

Utterance 1: Supportive of collaboration and improvement.

Utterance 2: Defensive and critical of perceived condescension.

No surprise either that the value it communicates is respect in dialogue, to be contrasted with the American high-level values such as 'human dignity':

Values

Utterance 1 emphasizes human dignity, human rights, and the benefits of collaboration.

Utterance 2 emphasizes respect, equality in dialogue, and cooperation.

The Chinese divergence can be better understood by considering the gap between the expressed values. The Chinese may ask themselves: How can you emphasize 'human dignity' when we experience disrespect in this dialogue? The same theme of respect appears in the analysis of principles.

Principles

Utterance 1: Collaboration, reinvention, and improvement.

Utterance 2: Respect for diplomatic protocols and equality in dialogue.

Here, we can deepen our understanding by noticing the different priorities.

Priorities

Utterance 1: International collaboration, progress, and innovation.
Utterance 2: Respectful dialogue and emphasis on cooperation.

Again, Sullivan is talking about high-level priorities, while the first Chinese priority is a respectful dialogue, as also emphasized in the tone.

Tone

Utterance 1: Confident, hopeful, and collaborative.
Utterance 2: Defensive, accusatory, and emphasizing equality.

Examining the differences in approach, historical context, and goals and objectives, the same theme repeats itself.

Approach

Utterance 1: Collaborative, open, and inclusive.
Utterance 2: Confrontational and emphasizing protocol.

Historical and Contextual References

Utterance 1: Recent achievements (Mars rover landing).
Utterance 2: Historical grievances and past diplomatic interactions.

Goals and Objectives

Utterance 1: Promote international collaboration, progress, and open dialogue.

Utterance 2: Ensure respectful and equal dialogue, emphasize cooperation, and address historical grievances.

Let me summarize what we have learned from the differences between the two utterances. Put simply, there are differences between the contents expressed by the two utterances. However, to recall, the

VPD represents how much the embedding v_2 is not aligned with the embedding v_1, or how much the embedding v_2 diverges from being a scaled version of the embedding v_1. So, the meaning of the divergence from differences is that it is much more difficult to understand the meaning of Yang's utterance through the abovementioned differences. It is as if pointing to the differences does not symmetrically help us to understand Yang and Sullivan. It is much more difficult to understand the Chinese. Even if we expose the differences, they do not symmetrically inform us of the speakers' perspectives. It is much more difficult to see the Chinese perspective through the differences. This raises the question of whether the same asymmetric divergence exists with respect to the similarities.

DIVERGENCE FROM SIMILARITY

Concerning the divergence from similarity, the greatest divergence was found between Blinken's second comment and Yang's first comment. This is also the case where the gap between the divergence from similarity and the divergence from difference was the greatest. The divergence from similarity expresses *the degree to which one interlocutor, in this case Blinken, does not reflect the common denominator with the other interlocutor.* Let me repeat: the VPD represents how much the embedding v_2 is not aligned with the embedding v_1 or how much the embedding v_2 diverges from being a scaled version of the embedding v_1. The embedding of Blinken's utterance is far more difficult to understand as a scaled version of the *similarities* between him and Yang. So, what does that mean? Let us analyze the similarities between the two utterances. The analysis of similarity with respect to the content categories shows the following.

For 'key issues,' both utterances:

> address the strategic dialogue between China and the United States,
>
> discuss the responsibilities of China and the United States in contributing to global peace, stability, and development,
>
> highlight economic achievements and development plans.

For 'stance,' both utterances:

emphasize the importance of sincere and candid dialogue,

assert their respective countries' positions on international relations and responsibilities.

For 'values,' both utterances:

mention the importance of peace, development, and justice,

discuss the significance of democracy and human rights in their contexts.

For 'principles,' both utterances:

underline adherence to international law and the U.N. Charter,

emphasize the need for mutual respect and cooperation.

For 'priorities,' both utterances:

prioritize enhancing bilateral relations and addressing global challenges like COVID-19 and climate change,

focus on promoting their own country's development and stability.

For 'tone,' both utterances:

maintain a formal and serious tone,

adopt a tone asserting their respective national perspectives and policies.

For 'approach,' both utterances:

advocate for a cooperative approach to international relations,

emphasize the need to manage differences through dialogue.

For 'historical and contextual references,' both utterances:

refer to past interactions and historical contexts to support their arguments,

mention significant historical achievements and events related to their countries.

For 'goals and objectives,' both utterances:

aim to enhance communication and cooperation between China and the United States,

aspire to achieve peace, stability, and development through their strategic dialogue.

It seems that the utterances are highly similar, so what are the differences? The differences are:

Key Issues

Utterance 1: Focuses on China's achievements, development plans, and criticism of the US actions.

Utterance 2: Emphasizes the US reengagement with allies and partners and concerns about China's actions.

Stance

Utterance 1: Adopts a defensive stance regarding criticism and promotes China's development model.

Utterance 2: Emphasizes US leadership and the quest for a more perfect union.

Values

Utterance 1: Highlights Chinese values aligning with humanity's common values.

Utterance 2: Stresses the US values of transparency, acknowledging imperfections, and striving for improvement.

Principles

Utterance 1: Advocates for China's model of peaceful development and non-interference.

Utterance 2: Emphasizes the US principles of confronting challenges openly and transparently.

Priorities

Utterance 1: Focuses on China's internal development goals and international contributions.

Utterance 2: Prioritizes the US reengagement with global allies and addressing global concerns about China's actions.

Tone

Utterance 1: Defensive and critical of the US actions.

Utterance 2: Assertive and confident about the US leadership and values.

Approach

Utterance 1: Emphasizes the need to abandon the Cold War mentality and zero-sum game approach.

Utterance 2: Highlights the importance of alliances and partnerships built on a voluntary basis.

Historical and Contextual References

Utterance 1: References China's historical achievements and five-year development plans.

Utterance 2: Mentions the US's historical approach to challenges and President Biden's past visit to China.

Goals and Objectives

Utterance 1: Aims to promote China's development model and criticize US interference.

Utterance 2: Seeks to reassure allies, address global concerns about China, and promote the US values of transparency and improvement.

The divergence of Blinken's utterance from the common grounds established by the similarities shows how it is much more difficult to understand Blinken through the similarities with the other side. Why? Probably because Blinken's utterance differs asymmetrically from the common denominator. Here, we return to the way our model and the divergence measure expose the asymmetry of perspectives. Even concerning similarities, we find an asymmetry between the speakers.

WHAT HAVE WE LEARNED?

What have we learned from using the LLM to understand diplomatic conversation? First, the model can expose implicit dimensions of the text, such as the ambiance and the situation. These dimensions are not explicitly mentioned in each utterance. We also learned that we can use these dimensions to enrich the original representation of the utterance. Finally, we showed that a simple measure of divergence can provide us with a numerical measure indicating the extent to which the perspective of one speaker diverges from another perspective represented by a different participant. Now, imagine an *AI agent* observing the meeting by analyzing the things said, the speakers' facial expressions, and their tone. The agent may also use external information resources to understand the people and the topics involved. For example, from Wikipedia, we learn that Blinken is a lawyer and an enthusiastic guitar player and that mentioning the conflict in Xinjiang to the Chinese is like weaving a red blanket in front of a nervous bull. This agent may integrate this information to analyze the conversation in real time. It may inform stakeholders about what is happening in the conversation and how to better adapt to the moves of the other participants.

SUMMARY

- The chapter introduces a novel approach for analyzing divergent perspectives in conversations, particularly in diplomatic discourse, using context-enriched embeddings generated by LLMs.
- It presents the VPD as a new metric to quantify the divergence between the perspectives of different speakers in a conversation, revealing significant asymmetries in diplomatic exchanges.
- The methodology enriches text embeddings with dimensions such as ambiance, situational dimensions, speech acts, and content categories, enhancing the depth and accuracy of conversation analysis.
- The effectiveness of this methodology is illustrated by analyzing the meeting between the US and Chinese officials, uncovering the underlying tensions and asymmetry of perspectives.
- I suggest finally that an AI agent equipped with this methodology could provide real-time insights during conversations by analyzing the text and other contextual information, improving strategic communication in high-stakes interactions.

NOTES

1 https://www.state.gov/secretary-antony-j-blinken-and-national-security-advisor-jake-sullivan-statements-to-the-press/
2 https://platform.openai.com/docs/guides/embeddings
3 https://blogs.nvidia.com/blog/what-is-retrieval-augmented-generation/
4 If required, normalize the divergence score by dividing it by the square root of the dimensionality of the vector.
5 To compare the divergence scores, I computed the median and the mean absolute deviation (MAD) and converted each score to NewScore = (score − median)/MAD.

REFERENCES

Neuman, Y. (2024). *AI for Understanding Context. Springer Brief in Computer Science.* New York, NY: Springer Nature.

Neuman, Y., & Cohen, Y. (2023). A dataset of 10,000 situations for research in computational social sciences psychology and the humanities. *Scientific Data, 10*(1), 505.

3

FRAMING CONVERSATIONS
WITH LLMs

EMPOWERING TECHNOLOGY WITH THEORY

In the opening chapter, I explained that large language models (LLMs) are sensitive to context. In the second chapter, I explained that their sensitivity can be significantly improved by prompting them to engage in certain forms of contextual analysis. Let me further explain and illustrate this point by analyzing a conversation from *Scenes from a Marriage*.[1] This was a TV drama written and directed by Ingmar Bergman. It is a masterpiece that presents the drama of married life, and in particular the crisis and disintegration of Marianne's and Johan's marriage. I urge you to watch the drama, freely available on YouTube.

The first scene is titled 'Innocence and Panic.' In this episode, Marianne and Johan are interviewed for a women's magazine, which presents them as the perfect married couple. The second scene begins with Johan and Marianne hosting a couple of friends, Peter and Katarina, for dinner. The scene opens with Johan reading a piece from the interview in which Marianne's eyes are described as being as blue as a folk song and lighting from within. Johan comments on this description, saying:

> One thing gets me: My eyes didn't get a mention. Don't they shine with a secret light?

DOI: 10.1201/9781003591047-3

Katerina responds by saying:

They're more like dark pools. The effect is quite sexy.

At this point, her husband Peter responds to his wife's utterance by addressing Johan and saying:

Katarina has a crush on you.

This slice of the conversation arises in an outwardly pleasant context where the participants are laughing and enjoying their drinks. Is it possible to understand the depth of the conversation using the model? To address this challenge, I draw on two theoretical constructs to prompt the model: framing and footing.

Erving Goffman's 'frame analysis' is a concept he developed to explain how people interpret and understand their experiences in social interactions. Goffman (1974) suggested that people use 'frames' to make sense of situations. These frames are mental structures or *schemes* that help individuals organize and interpret information. The idea of footing (Goffman, 1981) is concerned with the *participant's stance* in the conversation. As Goffman explains (Goffman, 1981, p. 128), it is the 'projected self' of the speaker, i.e., the way he presents who he is and the role he plays in the conversation.

I provided the model with a specific prompt using some general guidelines. One important guideline for prompting the model is breaking the task into sub-tasks or steps. Breaking a task into sub-tasks can help the model to perform. There are some platforms to support sub-tasking. For example, TaskGen[2] is "an open-sourced agentic framework which uses an agent to solve an arbitrary task by breaking them down into subtasks." In this book, I show how we can break a task into sub-tasks, using expert knowledge and a theoretically grounded approach. With respect to a sequence of actions that the model can perform, the platform LangChain[3] provides a framework for using LLMs in a sequential mode.

I first asked the model to identify the atmosphere of the conversation, then to identify the speech acts expressed by the utterance, and finally to analyze the conversation using the ideas of frame and footing.

Interestingly, the idea of framing, as originally proposed by Goffman, is vague. Therefore, I asked the model to propose guidelines for identifying the frame. This is an example of how the model can help us to understand theoretically vague concepts and propose guidelines on how to apply them. In contrast with the naïve idea of LLMs as input-output machines, they are participatory machines that can be involved in constructive dialogues. Understanding this aspect is key to the wise use of LLMs. Therefore, a second guideline is to approach the LLM as a partner for dialogue, and indeed a partner that is capable of reflecting and making improvements.

I thus incorporated the model's proposal and used the following prompt.

PROMPT 3.1

Analyze the following conversation by first identifying the **ambiance** expressed in the interaction. The **ambiance** refers to the mood, character, quality, tone, and atmosphere of the environment or milieu in which the conversation takes place.

Next, identify and categorize the **speech acts** expressed by each speaker.

Finally, interpret these speech acts using Erving Goffman's theory of **frames** and **footings**, with the identified ambiance as the background for the analysis.

Frames refer to the context or perspective through which the interaction is understood, while **footing** involves the roles, stances, and alignments that participants adopt during the conversation.

Step 1: Identify the ambiance

Mood and atmosphere: Determine the general mood and atmosphere of the conversation. Is it tense, playful, serious, affectionate, hostile, etc.?

Tone and quality: Consider the tone of the interaction—whether it's lighthearted, sarcastic, ominous, warm, etc.

Character of the interaction: Analyze the conversation's underlying character or emotional backdrop. Is there a sense of tension, vulnerability, irony, intimacy, etc.?

Step 2: Identify the speech acts

Categorize the speech acts: Identify the specific actions being performed through speech (e.g., assertion, question, command, compliment, complaint, etc.) by each speaker.

Relational dynamics: Consider how each speech act contributes to the relationship dynamics between the speakers.

Step 3: Analyze frames and footings (using ambiance as background)

Criteria for Identifying the Frame

Topic and content: Analyze the main topics each speaker introduces and the way they contextualize the conversation. Consider the conversation and the way each speaker's contributions shape the overall subject matter.

Purpose and intent: Consider the speaker's apparent purpose—whether they aim to inform, persuade, criticize, or negotiate. Identify how this intent contributes to framing the conversation within a specific context.

Implicit assumptions: Look for underlying assumptions that guide the conversation. For example, references to established norms, values, or shared understandings that implicitly define the boundaries of the discussion.

Shifts in focus: Monitor for shifts in the focus of the conversation, which may indicate a change in the frame. For instance, moving from specific issues to broader philosophical or ideological perspectives.

Criteria for Identifying the Footing

Speaker's role: Identify how the speaker positions themselves in the conversation (e.g., as an authority, a challenger, a supporter). This role is often reflected in their choice of words, tone, and the way they address others.

Tone and attitude: Analyze the tone of the speech—whether it's formal, informal, assertive, defensive, or conciliatory. The tone provides clues about the speaker's stance and the way they are positioning themselves in relation to the content and other participants.

Interactional alignment: Assess how the speaker aligns or distances themselves from others in the conversation. Determine whether they agree, disagree, support, or challenge others, as this reveals their relative footing.

Use of pronouns: Pay attention to the pronouns used (e.g., 'we,' 'I,' 'you,' 'they'), as they can indicate how the speaker is aligning themselves with others. For instance, 'we' might suggest collective alignment, while 'you' could imply a confrontational or directive stance.

Responsiveness to others: Observe how the speaker responds to previous statements, which may indicate shifts in footing. For example, a shift from neutrality to defensiveness can signify a change in stance or alignment.

Incorporate the ambiance into the frame and footing analysis: Use the identified ambiance as a lens to interpret the frames and footings. Consider how the mood and atmosphere influence the participants' roles, stances, and alignments. For example, a tense ambiance might lead to more defensive footings, while a playful ambiance might result in more fluid and shifting frames.

END

In response, the model generated the following output.

Ambiance Identification

Ambiance: The mood is a mix of playful flirtation and underlying tension. There is a sense of vulnerability in Johan's statement, sensuality in Katarina's response, and a hint of provocation in Peter's remark.

We see that the model correctly identified the ambiance. First, it identified the playful flirtation between Johan and Katarina. It also identified Johan's vulnerability. Complaining that his eyes did not receive any mention in the article seems like a humorous comment that amuses the others and no more. Surprisingly, the model identified a deeper layer underlying this utterance. This is quite interesting, as Johan presents himself as a highly confident extrovert in the first scene. Based on the humorous complaint, the model identified a hidden vulnerability that contrasts with the impression made by Johan. It seems that the model is intelligent enough to go beyond impression management.

The speech acts identified by the model are:

Johan
Complaint
Request for validation/compliment
Katarina
Disagreement/correction
Compliment
Peter
Assertion/statement

The next step involves the analysis of the utterances using Goffman's theory.

Frame: Johan frames the conversation in a personal and slightly insecure context, focusing on his insecurities and seeking validation. The ambiance of vulnerability and flirtation shapes this frame. Katarina reframes it toward a more intimate and flirtatious context, influenced by the sensual ambiance. Peter shifts the frame to relational tension by highlighting a potential romantic interest, using the underlying tension in the ambiance to provoke a reaction.

This frame analysis provides an interesting contextualization of Johan's utterance by pointing to a *psychological aspect of insecurity*. Katarina's utterance is framed through the *interpersonal dynamic of* flirtation. Flirtation is a playful way of showing sexual attraction and not a direct way of communicating it. As such, it is ambiguous, an important aspect, leaving space for withdrawal or denial of the attraction. In Chapter 8, I will discuss flirtation and ambiguity at length. Peter's response is framed as forming tension by clearing the ambiguity and exposing Katarina's sexual attraction.

Our understanding may be further enriched by the footing analysis generated by the model:

> **Footing**: Johan's footing is vulnerable and playful, seeking attention in line with the ambiance of flirtation and vulnerability. Katarina adopts a dominant and flirtatious footing, challenging Johan's self-perception and adding a layer of intimacy. Peter's footing is observational and slightly provocative, aligning with the ambiance of underlying tension to introduce a potential conflict or challenge.

Summarizing this analysis, we can describe the stances of the participants as follows:

Johan:	vulnerable and playful.
Katarina:	dominant and flirtatious.
Peter:	Provocative.

What we observe is the opening scene of a dinner conversation where the three interlocutors present different stances. Johan is vulnerable and playful, Katarina is assertive and flirtatious, and Peter is provocative. However, I have so far analyzed only the opening slice of the conversation. Later, the situation deteriorates into a bitter fight. But let us remain for the moment with the first part of the conversation, which is summarized by the model as follows:

> The conversation revolves around playful banter and underlying tensions among four characters—Johan, Marianne, Peter, and Katarina. Johan starts by seeking validation for his appearance, leading Katarina to flirt with him, which Peter humorously acknowledges. The conversation shifts to Marianne

defending Johan's fidelity while Peter and Katarina question his honesty in a lighthearted manner. The discussion briefly touches on professional achievements, revealing that Katarina had ghostwritten an article for Peter, highlighting their collaborative yet strained relationship. Despite the tension, the group toasts together, but the conversation ends with Johan urging them to avoid delving into life's injustices, signaling his desire for a more pleasant interaction.

Analyzing the first section of the conversation using the above prompt, the model provides the following output.

Ambiance

Mood and atmosphere: The conversation mixes **playfulness**, **tension**, and underlying **sarcasm**. There's an air of casual interaction, but it's laced with subtle jabs and emotional undercurrents.

Tone and quality: The tone is often **teasing** and **ironic**, with hints of **resentment** and **affection**. The characters engage in light banter, but the underlying tensions sometimes surface.

Character of the interaction: The interaction oscillates between **playful flirtation**, **sarcastic remarks**, and a sense of **discontent**. There's an emotional push and pull, with some moments of vulnerability masked by humor.

Despite the first impression of an enjoyable and humorous dinner, we can see that the model identifies the underlying currents and tensions. Tension, resentment, and sarcasm accompany the playful atmosphere. We next move to the model's analysis of speech acts.

Speech Acts

Johan

Complaint: "One thing gets me: My eyes didn't get a mention."

Request for validation/compliment: "Don't they shine with a secret light?"

Attempt to diffuse tension: "Let's try to have a pleasant time and not get into life's injustices."

We can see that the speech acts used by Johan tell us something interesting about him. He complains, seeks validation, and attempts to shift a topic to avoid the unpleasant tension. What frame can we adopt to integrate information about a person who uses such speech acts? I presented this question to the model and got the following answer:

1. **Insecurity or sensitivity**: The need to seek validation suggests that the person may be insecure or sensitive about how others perceive them. They might require external affirmation to feel confident or reassured.
2. **Desire for control**: By attempting to shift topics, especially away from uncomfortable or tense subjects, the person may try to maintain control over the conversation. This could indicate discomfort with vulnerability or confrontation, preferring to keep interactions within safe and manageable boundaries.
3. **Avoidance of conflict**: The combination of these speech acts suggests the person may be conflict-averse. They might prefer to deflect or steer away from difficult discussions rather than engage directly, indicating a possible reluctance to address underlying issues head-on.
4. **Self-focused behavior**: The tendency to complain and seek validation can also reveal a self-focused or introspective nature. This person might be more attuned to their needs and feelings, sometimes at the expense of broader social dynamics.

It is not necessarily the case that Johan is such a person, as his speech acts may not be representative. However, there are two interesting things to learn from the analysis. First, the insights into Johan's personality sharply contrast the way Johan presents himself in the interview and the way his wife, Marianne, perceives him. He is not as self-confident as he might seem but is insecure and vulnerable. In addition, the themes that appear in the first and the second scenes repeat themselves. Johan seems to be a self-centered and avoidant narcissist with a desire for control. Let's move to the speech acts used by the other characters.

Katarina

Correction/disagreement: "They're more like dark pools."

Compliment: "The effect is quite sexy."

Proposal (possibly sarcastic): "How about running off with me?"

Sarcastic response: "Well, I bet Johan is a better liar than you, my silly little darling."

Critique: "Peter embroiders his tales too much. It's almost touching."

Dismissal: "Nothing. Peter can be such a clod. That's all."

Analysis of her speech acts might suggest that Katarina is a sarcastic and critical woman. However, it is important to understand how speech acts are generated with respect to different participants. When addressing her husband, Katarina is sarcastic and dismissive, an approach that may strongly indicate the quality of their relationship. What about Marianne?

Marianne

Support: "A change would do Johan good. He's lived a married life for ten years, and he's never strayed."

Assurance: "Certainly. From the get-go I decided to believe everything Johan tells me."

Compliment: "I read your piece in Technical Times. Even I could understand it."

Inquiry: "Why does it have your byline?"

Concern: "What's wrong, Katarina?"

In contrast with Katarina, Marianne uses speech acts indicative of a different approach. She expresses confidence in Johan's loyalty to her and humorously supports the possibility of Johan's betrayal. She compliments Peter for an article he wrote and expresses concerns for Katarina's emotional state when facing Johan's bitter cruelty.

The analysis so far has provided a highly credible understanding of the situations and the participants. Moreover, in contrast with black box criticism of neural networks, the LLM provides a justified analysis. We can easily understand the analysis and the way the utterances support the conclusions.

In the next step, the model analyzes the frames and footings using ambiance as a background. The outcome of this analysis is as follows.

Frames and Footings (Using Ambiance as Background)
Frame

> **Johan** initially frames the conversation with a focus on his perceived slight, seeking validation in a lighthearted, slightly insecure way. The ambiance of **playful** tension influences this frame, where Johan's insecurity is masked by humor.

> **Katarina** reframes the interaction with a combination of flirtation and sarcasm. Her suggestion to "run off" and her correction of Johan's compliment steer the conversation toward a more intimate yet ironic context. The ambiance of tension and flirtation guides this frame, where emotions are expressed through layered sarcasm.

> **Peter** disrupts and reframes the conversation by making assertive and provocative statements, such as revealing that Katarina has a crush on Johan. This introduces a **competitive and confrontational frame**. The ambiance here becomes more charged with underlying tensions as Peter's remarks hint at deeper relational conflicts.

> **Marianne** attempts to frame the conversation in a **supportive and reassuring** context, but her remarks also carry subtle critiques. The ambiance of underlying discontent and support shapes this frame, where her words are meant to maintain harmony but also reflect the complexities of the relationships.

We can see how different frames guide the conversation. Peter's humorous reading of the article opens up the conversation but shifts to a flirtatious frame used by Katarina. This frame shares Johan's playfulness but shifts the conversation into a danger zone as her husband and Johan's wife are sitting before her. Picking up on this danger, Peter uses a confrontational frame. Marianne responds by shifting the frame into a more supportive and reassuring context. Our understanding deepens when we understand the footing in this slice of the conversation.

Footing

Johan first adopts a vulnerable and playful footing, seeking affirmation from others. As the conversation progresses, he shifts to a more **conciliatory footing** by attempting to diffuse tension and steer the group toward a more pleasant interaction, aligning with the ambiance of underlying tension.

Katarina maintains a **dominant and flirtatious footing**, using sarcasm and playful critiques to assert her position in the conversation. Her footing is influenced by the ambiance of tension and flirtation, where she balances between teasing and expressing deeper frustrations.

Peter's footing is more **provocative and self-deprecating**. He alternates between challenging others, revealing personal details, and mocking himself. This footing aligns with the ambiance of tension and sarcasm, as Peter uses humor to mask his insecurities and challenge the dynamics at play.

Marianne's footing is **supportive yet subtly critical**. She tries to maintain harmony and offer reassurance, but her questions and comments suggest underlying concerns or dissatisfaction. This footing is consistent with the ambiance of tension and discontent, where her supportive words are tinged with a recognition of the complexities in the relationships.

The footings identified by the model resonate with the previous analysis and give us an integrative understanding of the conversation. The overall analysis presented by the model is as follows:

> The conversation is characterized by playful tension, with moments of flirtation, sarcasm, and underlying discontent. Each speaker navigates this ambiance by adopting footings that allow them to express their emotions while maintaining a veneer of humor and lightheartedness. Johan's vulnerability is masked by humor, Katarina's flirtation is laced with sarcasm, Peter's provocations reveal deeper conflicts, and Mariana's support carries subtle critiques. The frames shift as each speaker attempts to steer the conversation in different directions, reflecting the complex dynamics of the interaction.

One must admit that the analysis provided by the model is remarkable in its depth. However, it should not be forgotten that I prompted the model and oriented it toward this analysis by guiding it through a sequence of theoretically grounded prompts. In my book on AI and context (Neuman, 2024), I used the term 'augmented intelligence' rather than 'artificial intelligence' to discuss the potential of LLMs. Augmented intelligence emphasizes technology as a tool for empowering human beings. The above analysis is an example of this approach. I prompt the model through my expertise, and in return, the model empowers my understanding. Instead of an input-output metaphor, we have a human being and a machine learning together in cycles of reflection and improvement. This point will be further explored in the next chapter, where I show how to incorporate memory and reflection into the process. But even in this chapter, we already see how working with an LLM in cycles where sub-tasks are designed through a theoretically oriented approach may enrich our understanding. Analyzing a dinner conversation within the context of a sophisticated drama, the model generated a deep and valid analysis. If you were provided with the full analysis without being told that an artificial mind created it, you would probably have mistaken it for an expert's analysis. In the past, passing the Turing test has been considered the ultimate criterion for intelligence. LLMs can easily pass the test. However, there is no need for philosophical discussions to use LLMs for a better understanding of human conversations. The proof of the pudding is in the eating, and so far, you have only tasted one bite of the pudding. The next chapters will provide some more.

SUMMARY

- The chapter demonstrates how Goffman's concepts of framing and footing can be applied to analyze conversations using LLMs, providing deep insights into interpersonal dynamics.
- By using a sequence of theoretically grounded prompts, the chapter shows how LLMs can be directed to perform nuanced analyses of conversations, revealing layers of meaning, mood, and social positioning that might not be immediately apparent.
- The analysis of a conversation from Ingmar Bergman's *Scenes from a Marriage* illustrates the interplay of moods, speech acts, and shifts in conversational frames, highlighting the complexity of human interactions and showing how LLMs can decode them.
- The chapter advocates for 'augmented intelligence,' where LLMs serve as tools to enhance human understanding rather than just executing tasks. The collaboration between human expertise and machine learning creates a cyclical process of reflection and improvement through dialogue with the machine.
- The analysis reveals how different characters in the conversation adopt various footings—vulnerability, flirtation, provocation, and subtle criticism—shaped by the ambiance, which in turn influences the frames and the direction of the conversation.

NOTES

1 https://en.wikipedia.org/wiki/Scenes_from_a_Marriage
2 https://github.com/simbianai/taskgen?tab=readme-ov-file
3 https://www.langchain.com/

REFERENCES

Goffman, E. (1974). *Frame Analysis: An Essay on the Organization of Experience*. New York, NY: Harper and Row.

Goffman, E. (1981). *Forms of Talk*. Pennsylvania, PA: University of Pennsylvania Press.

Neuman, Y. (2024). AI for Understanding Context. Springer Brief in Computer Science. New York, NY: Springer Nature.

4

TEACHING AI TO MEMORIZE CONVERSATIONS

THE IMPORTANCE OF MEMORY

Large language models (LLMs) are not accompanied by a component that preserves past interactions with users. Each time we open a query, we start from scratch. LLMs can be more powerful when provided with a memory of previous interactions with the user. Most examples in the literature use Chatbot learning to adapt to a specific user. For instance, assume that a user interacts with a Chatbot. Here is an example:

User:	I am looking for a good restaurant in Tel Aviv.
Chatbot:	How about a seafood restaurant?
User:	I only eat Kosher food

At this point, the Chatbot may recommend a Kosher restaurant in Tel Aviv, but unless provided with a memory, it may ignore the user's preference in the next interaction. Providing the model with a memory, the next interaction may look like this:

| User: | Please recommend a good restaurant in Berlin. |
| Chatbot: | Sure, let me look for Kosher restaurants in Berlin. |

DOI: 10.1201/9781003591047-4

Here, the chatbot remembers your specific dietary requirements and behaves accordingly. However, your preferences may change, and the model may learn and adapt accordingly:

User: I am now a Buddhist and only eat vegetarian food.
Chatbot: Let me look for a recommended vegetarian res-
                  taurant in Berlin.

An intelligent Chatbot not only remembers but also adapts its memory. However, the memory components of LLMs, such as the one used by Mem0[1] and other tools, are not easily adapted to human conversations. To illustrate this point, let me analyze a conversation in *Scenes from a Marriage*. To recall, in the first scene, Johan and Marianne are interviewed for a women's magazine. The scene is composed of 64 utterances. To better understand the following scenes, we may want to remember this opening scene of the drama. Representing all the utterances as they appear in the conversation is impractical and does not correspond to the way real people actually remember. Our memory is not a simple recording of the past but a device that represents the *meaning* of events and stores them for later use. The issue of meaning cannot be ignored, and simple summarization of declarative knowledge (i.e., knowledge of facts) by the memory component of some AI agents misses a crucial aspect of human memory. For instance, when introducing themselves to the journalist, Marriane and Johan generate the following utterances:

Marianne: "We've been married for ten years."
Johan: "Yes, I just renewed the contract."

Representing these utterances as pieces of declarative and procedural knowledge, we may get the following representations:

Utterance 1: Marianne: "We've been married for ten years."
   Predicate: BE-MARRIED
   Argument 1: Marianne, Johan

Argument 2: FOR-TIME

Argument 3: TEN-YEARS

Propositional Representation: BE-MARRIED (Marianne, Johan, FOR-TIME: TEN-YEARS)

Utterance 2: Johan: "Yes, I just renewed the contract."

Action: **RENEW-CONTRACT**

Subject: **Johan**

Object: **CONTRACT**

Time: **JUST**

Propositional Representation: **RENEW-CONTRACT (Johan, CONTRACT, JUST)**

These representations are correct and can be saved as memories, but do you see what they miss? First, not every utterance produced in the conversation is meaningful. The above memory device does not filter out less meaningful utterances. Second, it is not clear how to sort out meaningful utterances from less meaningful ones. When Marianne says that she and Johan have been married for ten years, she is not just mentioning a fact; she may be telling us something meaningful that is worth representing in the memory of the conversation. To understand what a meaningful memory is, let us analyze the memories Marianne and Johan recall during the interview. What we do here puts into practice the idea of dialoguing with the machine. Rather than a human being arriving with full knowledge of the situation or a machine that takes all responsibility for doing the work, I try to work in concert with the machine to better understand the nature of human memory.

One may wonder why I do not simply use the vast amount of memory research in psychology instead of dialoguing with a machine. But the problem is that too much psychological research cannot be trusted. It is not only the reproducibility crisis in psychology (Open Science Collaboration, 2015), but also the low 'face validity' and 'ecological validity' of psychological research that makes it hard to trust. Put simply, the organization and norms in psychology do not meet the standards of scientific thinking.

To give but one example, in a highly cited paper by a 'leading light' in the world of psychology, Dan Ariely, subjects were manipulated to write down either the names of ten books they had read or the Ten Commandments. The researchers 'found' that subjects did not cheat after taking part in the Ten Commandments recall task. Hallelujah! But this finding lacks any serious scientific grounding, and the fact that it was published and popularized is a mystery to the scientific-oriented mind. However, I suspect that I understand why, despite the shaken validity of this finding, the lead researcher turned out to be a star. In a Christian culture where acknowledging Jesus as a savior is enough for redemption, recalling the Ten Commandments may be a sufficient condition for influencing people's moral behavior. While I am writing this book, we are still in a war with the terror organization of Hamas, which invaded Israel, murdered, beheaded, burned, raped, and kidnapped Israeli citizens, including young children and babies. Unfortunately, the highly cited paper by Ariely (3887 citations!) did not gain enough attention from the Israeli military command, who could apparently have prevented the attack simply by putting signs with the Ten Commandments on the fence along the Israeli border, reminding Hamas of their moral duties as the sons of Abraham ...

I hope my sarcasm has been well taken. Returning, then, to the question of memory, it will be useful to begin by presenting a summary of the conversation.

A HAPPY COUPLE?

The conversation begins with the journalist, Mrs. Palm, initiating the interview with Johan and Marianne, asking them to describe themselves. Johan provides an extensive, somewhat self-aggrandizing description, mentioning his attributes (e.g., sexy) and accomplishments. At the same time, Marianne offers a more reserved response, primarily focused on her role as Johan's wife and the mother of their daughters. The conversation touches on their family backgrounds, professions, and how they met, with Johan and Marianne recounting their early relationships, their eventual union, and how they grew to love each other. Despite portraying themselves as a nearly perfect couple with a stable and contented life, there is a subtle acknowledgment of underlying tensions and the potential dangers of their seemingly problem-free existence. Johan expresses a somewhat cynical view of the world, contrasting with Marianne's belief in compassion and caring for others. The conversation is punctuated by Mrs. Palm's instructions to hold poses for the camera, adding an element of formality and performance to the exchange.

Given this context, let us return to analyzing the opening utterances. When Johan suggests that they 'just renewed' their contract, this memory corresponds to Marianne's first utterance, asserting that they have been married for ten years. This memory is only one illustration of how memories are *discursively evoked* in a conversation. In daily life, memories do not randomly pop up. They are usually evoked in a dynamic and discursive context. Therefore, Johan, by mentioning the 'renewal' of their marriage contract, aligns himself with Marianne's utterance.

We can use Goffman's ideas to understand the meaning of these memories and the way they popped up in the conversation. More specifically, using Goffman's frame theory, we can analyze Johan and Marianne's recollections of past events by examining the frames they use to interpret and present their past experiences. The analysis will focus on how these frames shape their understanding of their relationship, how they present themselves to others, and how they negotiate their shared history in the conversation. This approach differs from the psychological one for identifying patterns in human memories. I first automatically identify the memories, then try to identify patterns in these memories. I thus use a 'grounded' approach for identifying patterns in the way memories are used in the conversation.

I began by asking the model to analyze the recollection of past events using Goffman's frame theory. Here is the output generated for the two utterances (my emphasis):

Marianne: "We've been married for ten years."
> **Frame**: This statement is framed within a temporal context that emphasizes *stability* and duration. The mention of 'ten years' frames a long-term, committed relationship.

Footing: Marianne takes a reflective stance, positioning herself as someone who values the longevity of their marriage.
This creates a frame of continuity and resilience in their
relationship.

The LLM suggests something interesting. Marianne's choice of mentioning that they have been married for ten years is not arbitrary.
It is a choice, probably unconscious, that emphasizes the *stability* of
their relationship. Memories, similar to speech acts, are functional
moves. Framing the memory allows us to contextualize and instill
it with meaning. Marianne recalls the long duration of their relationship because it is important to her to present the stability of that
relationship. The frame is one of stability, and the stance emphasizes
her projected self as she mentions the past. This is how she tries
to present herself and her husband to the journalist. This interpretation allows us to get a better understanding of the 'footing' or
stance communicated by Marianne. Marianne presents herself as a
person who values stability. We should remember this when trying
to understand future conversations in which Marianne is involved.
But what about Johan?

Johan: "Yes, I just renewed the contract."
  Frame: Johan reinterprets the marriage in a bureaucratic or
    contractual frame, which contrasts with the emotional
    and personal frame that Marianne initially sets. This intro-
    duces a frame of formality and perhaps a hint of irony or
    detachment.
  Footing: Johan's footing shifts to a more playful or cynical
    stance, possibly indicating a more distanced or pragmatic
    view of their relationship.

Johan's utterance seems to correspond to Marianne's, but the LLM
points out the *contrast* between the frames. Johan responds to Marianne's
utterance by *distancing* himself from emotion and thus presenting himself as more emotionally detached. In fact, he *shifts* the frame to a
bureaucratic or contractual one, contrasting with Marianne's more

emotional and personal frame. This could imply a pragmatic or even slightly ironic view of their marriage. Remembering the conversation in order to inform future conversations, we may record Marianne as being a woman who cherishes stability and Johan as emotionally detached and somehow critical of Marianne. At this point, we may want to inquire more deeply into memories formed in a conversation by identifying all references to past events and identifying themes in the evoked memories. These themes may help us to understand how to prompt the LLM to store traces of past conversations in a way that is aligned with the way human memories work in a conversation.

WHY ARE CERTAIN MEMORIES EVOKED IN A CONVERSATION?

To better understand why some memories are evoked, we prompt the model to identify the reasons for recalling certain things. However, as explained in the previous chapter, we break the task into a sequence of sub-tasks to make it easier for the model. The first sub-task is to identify utterances concerning past events.

PROMPT 4.1

Sub-task 1: Identify utterances mentioning past events

Instructions

Analyze the given conversation.

Past tense of verbs: Identify utterances that use past tenses of verbs (e.g., 'was,' 'did,' 'had,' 'went') to signal references to past events.

Temporal markers: Pay attention to temporal markers such as 'ago,' 'yesterday,' 'last,' or specific past times, which indicate references to past events.

Contextual indicators: Consider the context of the conversation to identify when a speaker is discussing something that has already happened, even if the verb tense is not explicitly past.

> Cross-check for accuracy: Cross-check potential past event references with the surrounding context to ensure they accurately reflect past experiences.
>
> Verify speaker attribution: Double-check the speaker for each identified past event by reviewing the flow of the conversation, ensuring the correct attribution of each utterance.
>
> Present the list of utterances mentioning past events.
>
> END

The model correctly identified 13 utterances mentioning past events. They are described as follows:

> Marianne mentions that their marriage has lasted for a decade.
>
> Johan humorously comments that he has recently reaffirmed their marriage.
>
> Marianne explains that she is the youngest of seven siblings and that her mother, who used to manage a big household, now has a more relaxed life.
>
> Johan describes their relationship history, noting that they didn't fall in love immediately.
>
> Johan reflects that there was initially little mutual interest between them.
>
> Marianne recalls that Johan was romantically involved with a famous pop singer then.
>
> Johan mentions that Marianne, at 19, was married to a young man who mainly benefited from having a wealthy father.
>
> Marianne notes that her first husband was very kind and that she was deeply in love with him.
>
> Marianne adds that she became pregnant during that marriage.
>
> Marianne shares that her baby passed away shortly after birth, leading to her and her husband's separation.
>
> Johan mentions that the pop singer broke up with him.
>
> Marianne says they realized they got along very well, so their academic performance improved.

Marianne explains that they thought their mothers would be shocked by their decision to live together, but they weren't.

Marianne adds that their mothers quickly became close friends.

Johan notes that they had fallen in love by that time.

Marianne emphasizes that they were deeply in love.

Johan comments that others perceived them as the ideal couple.

Marianne recalls hearing that a lack of problems in a relationship could actually lead to conflicts.

Using these utterances, I asked the model to identify the frames involved in them:

PROMPT 4.2

Sub-task 2. Identify the frame used to present the memory in a given utterance

Task: Use Goffman's frame analysis to identify the frame used to present a memory

Instructions

Analyze the list of utterances mentioning past events.

##

For the analysis, use Goffman's ideas of FRAME ANALYSIS and FOOTING.

Footing refers to the alignment or stance individuals adopt in an interaction, which can shift depending on the context or the frames in play. It concerns the way a speaker positions themselves in relation to the other participants and the ongoing interaction.

Frame analysis is a method for understanding how people interpret and make sense of their social interactions. It involves examining the mental frameworks, or 'frames,' that participants use to organize and structure their experiences during a conversation. These frames guide behavior, influence communication, and shape the dynamics of the interaction.

##

Frame recognition: Identify the frame used in each utterance.

Frame purpose: Understand the general purpose of the frame. For instance, is the speaker trying to establish credibility, evoke empathy, or manage social perceptions?

Footing recognition: Identify the footing or stance expressed by the utterance given the frame.

END

Here are two outputs provided by the model:

Utterance: Marianne mentions that she and Johan have been married for a decade.

Frame recognition: Personal history frame—Marianne recounts a fact from their shared history, framing it as a long-term commitment.

Frame purpose: To establish the longevity and stability of their marriage.

Footing recognition: Marianne adopts a stance of shared experience and commitment within the interaction, positioning herself as part of a long-term partnership.

Utterance: Johan explains that when Marianne was 19, she married a young man whose primary advantage was having a wealthy father.

Frame recognition: Critical evaluation frame—Johan offers an evaluative judgment of Marianne's previous marriage.

Frame purpose: To provide a critical perspective on Marianne's past relationship, possibly contrasting it with their current relationship.

Footing recognition: Johan assumes a judgmental and slightly dismissive stance, positioning himself as a commentator on Marianne's past decisions.

Next, and drawing on the outcome of the previous analysis, I prompt the model to identify the speakers' intentions when evoking a memory:

PROMPT 4.3

Sub-task 3. Analyze the speaker's intentions

Task: Identify the reason why a specific memory is evoked in the conversation.

Explaining the task: During a conversation, memories may be evoked for several reasons. Here are some reasons:

Establishing a Shared Frame of Reference

Memories are often evoked to create a common understanding or context between participants. By referencing past events, individuals align their frames, ensuring everyone shares the same background or narrative context for the given interaction.

Reinforcing Social Identity and Roles

Memories help to reinforce social identities and roles within a conversation. By recalling specific events, individuals can emphasize their role in a relationship or social group, affirming their position and its expectations.

Managing Social Perception and Impression

Individuals evoke memories to manage how others perceive them. By selecting specific memories that highlight desirable traits or experiences, they can control the frame through which others view them, projecting an image that aligns with their social goals.

Negotiating Power and Control

In social interactions, evoking certain memories can serve as a way to assert control over the conversation. By framing the past in a particular way, a speaker can influence the direction of the interaction, establishing dominance or guiding the narrative.

Aligning or Shifting Footing

Recalling memories can be a strategy to align or shift footing within a conversation. By referencing the past, individuals can change the stance they take in the interaction, either drawing closer to the other participants or distancing themselves, depending on the desired outcome.

Emphasizing Continuity or Change

Memories highlight the continuity or change in a person's life or in a relationship. By framing past events in a certain way, individuals can either reinforce the idea that things have remained stable or emphasize how much has changed, depending on the narrative they want to construct.

Addressing or Deflecting Emotional Content

Evoking memories can serve either to address emotional content directly or to deflect it. For example, recalling a happy memory might be used to diffuse tension, while a more painful memory might be brought up to address underlying emotions that need to be acknowledged.

Creating a Narrative Arc

Memories are often used to construct a coherent narrative within a social interaction. By framing the past as part of a larger story, individuals can give structure to the conversation, making sense of the present and guiding the anticipated future.

Building or Reaffirming Social Bonds

Sharing memories can strengthen social bonds by highlighting shared experiences and common history. This helps to create a sense of connection and mutual understanding, reinforcing the social fabric of the relationship.

Resolving or Acknowledging Conflict

In some cases, memories are evoked to resolve or acknowledge conflict within a social interaction. By recalling past events, individuals can frame the conflict to mitigate tension or bring unresolved issues to the forefront for discussion.

##

Instructions

Use the output of the previous frame analysis.

Identify the speech act underlying the utterance.

For each utterance mentioning a past event, use the frame analysis, footing, and speech act to identify the reason why the memory is evoked.

END

The outcome of this analysis includes the following explanations:

1. For the utterance where Marianne mentions that she and Johan have been married for a decade:

   Frame analysis: Personal history frame—Marianne recounts a fact from their shared history.

   Footing: Marianne takes a stance of shared experience and commitment.

   Speech act: Asserting a shared history.

   Reason for evoking memory: Establishing a shared frame of reference—Marianne evokes this memory to create a common understanding of their long-term commitment, aligning the frame of reference between herself, Johan, and the interviewer.

   For the utterance where Johan says that Marianne was married to a boy whose only virtue was a rich father:

   Frame analysis: Critical evaluation frame—Johan offers an evaluative judgment of Marianne's previous marriage.

   Footing: Johan assumes a judgmental and slightly dismissive stance.

   Speech act: Critiquing past relationships.

Reason for evoking memory: Reinforcing social identity and roles—Johan evokes this memory to reinforce his current role in Marianne's life, contrasting it with her past relationships to emphasize his superiority or the depth of their current relationship.

We see that, by considering two memories, the model identified two explanations: establishing a shared frame of reference and reinforcing social identities and roles. Using this approach, we can analyze all the memories evoked in the conversation and identify patterns in the way memories are used.

At this point, we may want to generalize the findings to understand the participants and their relationships on the basis of their recollection of past events:

PROMPT 4.4

Assume that I would like to understand Johan and Marianne better. Use the above analysis and its outcomes and briefly explain who Johan and Marianne are and their relationship.

END

The model summarizes the findings as follows:

Johan and Marianne are a married couple who have been together for over a decade, and their relationship is marked by a mix of humor, shared history, and underlying complexities. Johan often uses humor and a relaxed demeanor to manage how he is perceived, subtly guiding the narrative to maintain control and projecting confidence and ease. On the other hand, Marianne reveals a more reflective and emotionally nuanced side, addressing past traumas and concerns while affirming her contentment with their life together. Their interactions suggest a deep bond forged through shared experiences and mutual support but hint at underlying tensions and emotional layers that complicate their seemingly stable relationship. Together, they present a dynamic where Johan often takes the lead in shaping the conversation. At the same time, Marianne provides depth and emotional context, highlighting both the strengths and challenges of their long-term partnership.

Based on the memory patterns, the model has identified some interesting things about the speakers. However, is it the best we can do? To answer this question, let me illustrate the model's ability to reflect and improve through my mediation as its mentor and student.

IMPROVING THE MODEL THROUGH REFLECTION

The model provides a nice analysis and integration of the memories and how they may enrich our understanding of the speakers. However, we can do better through *reflection*. The model can reflect on its output and improve it. Therefore, I've asked the model to do just this and provide instructions that would give a better output.

PROMPT 4.5

I would like your explanation to better inform our understanding of future conversations involving Johan and Marianne. Given this context, reflect on your explanation. In addition, use your reflection to propose improved instructions for generating a better understanding of Johan, Marianne, and their relationship.
END

The model responded as follows.

Proposed Instructions for Future Conversations

Identify the Individual Motivations

For each speaker, identify the motivations behind their speech acts, especially focusing on humor, irony, and emotional disclosures. Analyze how these elements reflect their underlying emotional states and goals in the conversation.

Analyze the Power Dynamics

Track shifts in control and influence within the conversation. Identify who is leading the interaction, how they maintain control, and how the other speaker responds to or challenges this dynamic.

Contextualize Conversations with Past Experiences

Relate the conversation to past events and experiences, noting how these memories reinforce or challenge current roles, identities, and perceptions within the relationship.

Explore the Emotional Depth

Pay close attention to moments of emotional expression, whether overt or subtle. Analyze how these emotions impact the interaction and what they reveal about the relationship's deeper layers.

Consider Social and Public Perception

Evaluate how Johan and Marianne manage their social identities in the conversation. Consider how their awareness of external perceptions influences their communication and relationship dynamics.

I accepted the model's proposed instructions and asked it to complete the final task.

PROMPT 4.6

Please apply these improved instructions. Based on the analysis so far, provide a short paragraph explaining who Johan and Marianne are and their relationship. This paragraph will be used to analyze future conversations in which Johan and Marianne are involved.

END

The model provided the following output:

> Johan and Marianne are a married couple with a long history marked by shared experiences, emotional depth, and underlying complexities. Johan often uses humor and a controlled demeanor to manage social perceptions, maintain narrative control, and possibly mask deeper insecurities. He subtly guides conversations, positioning himself as confident and detached. Marianne, in contrast, is reflective and emotionally aware, often addressing underlying tensions or past traumas that influence their relationship. She balances Johan's control with her candidness, revealing their bond's emotional layers. Their relationship dynamics involve a continuous negotiation of power, shaped by their past experiences and how they present themselves both publicly and privately. This nuanced interplay between control, emotional depth, and shared history will be crucial in analyzing their future interactions.

This is an excellent description of the speakers and a meaningful description that we can use as a memory for understanding future conversations between the two. However, I would like to gain an understanding of human memories in general, so I asked the model the following question.

PROMPT 4.7

Imagine that you are a human being listening to the conversation. Based on the analysis you presented so far, what key points will you remember from the conversation?
END

The model responded as follows:

> If I were a human being listening to the conversation, the key points I would remember based on the analysis are:
>
> 1. **Longevity of marriage**: Johan and Marianne have been married for ten years, a significant milestone that they both acknowledge, though Johan does so with humor, referring to it as renewing a contract.

2. **Johan's use of humor**: Johan consistently uses humor and irony to manage the tone of the conversation, possibly to maintain control and mask deeper emotions. This includes joking about their marriage as a contract and lightly dismissing the seriousness of past events.

3. **Marianne's reflectiveness**: Marianne is more emotionally expressive and reflective, sharing personal and sometimes painful memories, such as the loss of her first child, which influenced the start of her relationship with Johan. Her reflections reveal underlying emotional layers in their relationship.

4. **Power dynamics**: Johan subtly guides the conversation, often positioning himself as the more detached and confident partner. At the same time, Marianne occasionally challenges this dynamic with her candidness and emotional depth.

5. **Shared history and social perception**: Johan and Marianne are aware of how they are perceived by each other and others. They reference past experiences to manage these perceptions, such as Johan's past publicized relationship with a pop singer and how they were viewed as the perfect couple.

6. **Underlying tensions**: Despite the humor and the apparent stability in their relationship, there are hints of underlying tensions, such as Marianne's mention of how the lack of problems could cause strife, suggesting that not everything is as perfect as it seems.

These key points proposed by the model can be used as a memory to inform our analysis of future conversations in which Johan and Marianne are involved. Now, we can analyze the following scene involving the dinner conversation with a proper context resulting from the memory of the previous conversation in which Johan and Marianne have been involved. Let us return to the dinner scene and try to understand it through the memory of the first scene.

REANALYZING THE DINNER CONVERSATION USING MEMORY

I used the following prompt that drew on the memory of the previous scene.

PROMPT 4.8

Please analyze the following conversation.
##

The conversation involves the following participants: Johan, Marianne, Peter, and Katarina.
##

Background information on Johan and Marianne:

1. Longevity of marriage: Johan and Marianne have been married for ten years, a significant milestone that they both acknowledge, though Johan does so with humor, referring to it as renewing a contract.

2. Johan's use of humor: Johan consistently uses humor and irony to manage the tone of the conversation, possibly to maintain control and mask deeper emotions. This includes joking about their marriage as a contract and lightly dismissing the seriousness of past events.

3. Marianne's reflectiveness: Marianne is more emotionally expressive and reflective, sharing personal and sometimes painful memories, such as the loss of her first child, which influenced the start of her relationship with Johan. Her reflections reveal underlying emotional layers in their relationship.

4. Power dynamics: Johan tends to subtly guide the conversation, often positioning himself as the more detached and confident partner, while Marianne occasionally challenges this dynamic with her candidness and emotional depth.

5. Shared history and social perception: Both Johan and Marianne are aware of how they are perceived, both by

each other and by others. They reference past experiences to manage these perceptions, such as Johan's past publicized relationship with a pop singer and how they were viewed as the perfect couple.

6. Underlying tensions: Despite the humor and the apparent stability in their relationship, there are hints of underlying tensions, such as Marianne's mention of how the lack of problems could cause strife, suggesting that not everything is as perfect as it seems.

##

The conversation is:

Johan:	One thing gets me: My eyes didn't get a mention. Don't they shine with a secret light?
Katerina:	They're more like dark pools. The effect is quite sexy.
Peter:	Katarina has a crush on you.

##

Instruction for the analysis:

Use the background information to analyze the conversation.

Analyze the conversation by first identifying the ambiance expressed in the interaction. Ambiance refers to the mood, character, quality, tone, and atmosphere of the environment or milieu in which the conversation takes place.

Next, identify and categorize the speech acts expressed by each speaker.

Finally, interpret these speech acts using Erving Goffman's theory of frames and footings, with the identified ambiance as the background for the analysis.

Frames refer to the context or perspective through which the interaction is understood, while footing involves the roles, stances, and alignments that participants adopt during the conversation.

Step 1: Identify the ambiance

Mood and atmosphere: Determine the general mood and atmosphere of the conversation. Is it tense, playful, serious, affectionate, hostile, etc.?

Tone and quality: Consider the tone of the interaction—whether it's lighthearted, sarcastic, ominous, warm, etc.

Character of the interaction: Analyze the conversation's underlying character or emotional backdrop. Is there a sense of tension, vulnerability, irony, intimacy, etc.?

Step 2: Identify the speech acts

Categorize speech acts: Identify the specific actions being performed through speech (e.g., assertion, question, command, compliment, complaint, etc.) by each speaker.

Relational dynamics: Consider how each speech act contributes to the relationship dynamics between the speakers.

Step 3: Analyze frames and footings (using ambiance as background)

Criteria for identifying the frame:

Topic and content: Analyze the main topics each speaker introduces and the way they contextualize the conversation. Consider the conversation and the way each speaker's contributions shape the overall subject matter.

Purpose and intent: Consider the speaker's apparent purpose—whether they aim to inform, persuade, criticize, or negotiate. Identify how this intent contributes to framing the conversation within a specific context.

Implicit assumptions: Look for underlying assumptions that guide the conversation. For example, references to established norms, values, or shared understandings that implicitly define the boundaries of the discussion.

Shifts in focus: Monitor for shifts in the focus of the conversation, which may indicate a change in the frame. For

instance, moving from specific issues to broader philosophical or ideological perspectives.

Criteria for identifying the footing:

Speaker's role: Identify how the speaker positions themselves
in the conversation (e.g., as an authority, a challenger, a supporter). This role is often reflected in their choice of words,
tone, and the way they address others.

Tone and attitude: Analyze the tone of the speech—whether
it's formal, informal, assertive, defensive, or conciliatory.
The tone provides clues about the speaker's stance and how
they are positioning themselves in relation to the content
and other participants.

Interactional alignment: Assess how the speaker aligns or
distances themselves from others in the conversation.
Determine whether they agree, disagree, support, or challenge others, as this reveals their relative footing.

Use of pronouns: Pay attention to the pronouns used (e.g.,
'we,' 'I,' 'you,' 'they'), as they can indicate how the speaker
is aligning themselves with others. For instance, 'we' might
suggest collective alignment, while 'you' could imply a
confrontational or directive stance.

Responsiveness to others: Observe how the speaker responds
to previous statements, which may indicate shifts in footing. For example, a shift from neutrality to defensiveness
can signify a change in stance or alignment.

Incorporate ambiance into frame and footing analysis: Use the
identified ambiance as a lens to interpret the frames and footings. Consider how the mood and atmosphere influence the
participants' roles, stances, and alignments. For example, a tense
ambiance might lead to more defensive footings, while a playful ambiance might result in more fluid and shifting frames.

##

In your analysis, be specific about the way the background
information on Johan and Marianne informs your analysis

END

The model provided the following analysis.

Step 1: Identify the Ambiance

Mood and Atmosphere

The mood of the conversation is lighthearted and playful. Johan's comment about his eyes shining with a secret light introduces a tone of self-aware humor, which Katarina picks up on by describing his eyes as "dark pools" and adding that the effect is "quite sexy." Peter's comment about Katarina having a crush on Johan further enhances the playful and teasing atmosphere.

Tone and Quality

The tone of the conversation is flirtatious yet controlled, with underlying layers of irony. Johan's humor is self-deprecating yet subtly flattering, and Katarina's response is complimentary but slightly exaggerated, adding to the light, flirtatious banter. Peter's remark adds a slightly provocative note to the interaction, playfully implying something more in Katarina's compliment.

The Character of the Interaction

The interaction carries an undercurrent of irony and controlled vulnerability. Johan uses humor as a shield, masking any deeper emotions that might be associated with being complimented. Katarina's playful flirtation subtly challenges Johan's control over the conversation. Peter's interjection encourages this challenge, suggesting that Johan may not be as much in control as he appears.

Step 2: Identify the speech acts

Johan

Speech Act: Assertion
>
> Action: Johan asserts his awareness of his appearance, particularly his eyes, but does so humorously to manage the tone and possibly to invite compliments in a non-serious manner.

Relational dynamics: Johan's humor sets the stage for a light-hearted interaction, where he positions himself as someone who can take a compliment but doesn't need it, subtly controlling the interaction.

Katarina

Speech Act: Compliment
Action: Katarina compliments Johan's eyes, describing them as 'dark pools' with a 'sexy' effect. This form of playful flirtation matches Johan's humorous tone and adds a layer of intimacy.
Relational dynamics: Katarina's compliment shifts the power slightly as she engages Johan on a more personal level. It's a subtle challenge to Johan's control, introducing a moment of vulnerability that Johan's humor had initially masked.

Peter

Speech Act: Assertion
Action: Peter asserts that Katarina has a crush on Johan, framing her compliment as more than playful banter. His statement adds a layer of provocation, suggesting a deeper underlying tension or attraction.
Relational dynamics: Peter's remark disrupts the balance Johan had created, suggesting that there may be more emotional depth beneath the surface. This comment could potentially shift the dynamic between Johan and Katarina, as it brings an element of seriousness to the otherwise lighthearted conversation.

Step 3: Analyze Frames and Footings

Frames

Topic and content: The conversation revolves around Johan's appearance, specifically his eyes. Johan frames the discussion with humor, keeping it light and controlled. While matching his humor, Katarina subtly reframes it by introducing a more flirtatious and intimate perspective. Peter then reframes the conversation by suggesting that Katarina's compliment might have deeper implications, adding a layer of seriousness to the interaction.

Purpose and intent: Johan's intent is to maintain a lighthearted, humorous tone, potentially to avoid revealing any deeper vulnerabilities. Katarina's intent seems to be to engage Johan more personally, adding flirtation to the mix. Peter's intent appears to provoke, adding complexity to the interaction by suggesting a possible hidden attraction.

Implicit assumptions: The conversation assumes a shared understanding of humor and flirtation. Johan's humor is expected to be understood as non-serious, and Katarina's compliment as playful. Peter's interjection assumes that the others will pick up on the underlying tension he is pointing out.

Shifts in focus: The conversation shifts from a lighthearted joke about Johan's appearance to a more flirtatious exchange and then to a potentially more serious consideration of the implications of that flirtation. This shift indicates a change in the frame from playful banter to a more complex interaction with potential emotional depth.

Footing

Speaker's Role

Johan: Positions himself as the humorous, self-aware participant who controls the tone of the conversation.

Katarina: Takes on a flirtatious role, subtly challenging Johan's control by engaging with him more intimately.

Peter: Positions himself as an observer and provocateur, disrupting the existing dynamic and introducing the possibility of deeper emotions.

Tone and Attitude

Johan: Uses a light, humorous tone to maintain control and avoid vulnerability.

Katarina: Adopts a playful, flirtatious tone, engaging with Johan's humor and adding a layer of intimacy.

Peter: Takes on a slightly provocative tone, suggesting a shift from playful banter to something more serious.

Interactional Alignment

Johan: Aligns himself with a position of control, using humor to manage the interaction.

Katarina: Aligns herself with Johan initially through humor but then subtly shifts to challenge his control through flirtation.

Peter: Aligns himself as an outsider who observes and comments, potentially shifting the dynamic by suggesting deeper implications.

Use of Pronouns

Johan: Uses 'my' to focus on himself and maintain control.

Katarina: Uses 'they' and 'quite' to compliment Johan, focusing on him and adding intimacy.

Peter: Uses 'you' to directly address Johan, emphasizing the personal nature of the interaction.

Responsiveness to Others

Johan: Responds to his appearance humorously, avoiding deeper emotional engagement.

Katarina: Responds to Johan's humor with a compliment that adds a flirtatious layer, subtly challenging his control.

Peter: Responds to the entire interaction with a comment that disrupts the existing dynamic, suggesting a shift in footing from lighthearted to potentially more serious.

Incorporating Ambiance into the Frame and Footing Analysis

The playful and ironic ambiance allows Johan to maintain his controlled footing, using humor to avoid deeper emotional engagement. However, this ambiance also enables Katarina to challenge his control through flirtation, introducing an element of intimacy that shifts the frame. While still within the lighthearted ambiance, Peter's comment adds a hint of seriousness that could lead to a further shift in the footing, potentially revealing underlying tensions or emotions.

The background information about Johan's use of humor, Marianne's reflectiveness, and their shared history informs this analysis by highlighting Johan's tendency to use humor as a defense mechanism and Katarina's potential to challenge this control through more emotionally engaging interactions. Peter's role as a provocateur adds complexity to this dynamic, suggesting that the lightheartedness of the conversation may be masking deeper tensions.

What are the differences between the memory-informed analysis and the previous analysis? The differences between the memory-informed analysis and the other are as follows:

Ambiance Analysis

With background: Identifies a controlled, ironic tone with underlying vulnerability and tension.

Without background: Describes a straightforward, playful, teasing mood without deeper layers.

Speech Acts Analysis

With background: Interprets Johan's humor as a control mechanism; sees Katerina's response as subtly challenging his control; views Peter's comment as potentially introducing deeper tension.

Without background: Sees Johan's remark as simple validation-seeking; Katerina's response as straightforward flirtation; Peter's comment as lighthearted teasing.

Frame Analysis

With background: Frames the conversation as involving subtle power dynamics and potential shifts toward deeper emotional engagement.

Without background: Frames the conversation as playful banter and flirtation without deeper implications.

Footing Analysis

With background: Highlights Johan's guarded control, Katerina's challenge, and Peter's role as a potential destabilizer.

Without background: Emphasizes all participants maintaining a playful, non-threatening footing.

Incorporation of Ambiance

With background: Suggests that the ambiance masks deeper emotional undercurrents.

Without background: Treats the ambiance as straightforward, reinforcing playful interactions without hidden tensions.

We can see that memory-informed analysis adds some depth to the analysis of this thin slice of the conversation. We can now understand how to better inform the model by providing a memory of past interactions. It is important to remember that this memory is not a simple recording of past events. It is a memory based on the way real people keep track of previous conversations and the way such conversations can inform them about the participants and their social dynamics. This is just a particular instance of the way human memory works. For example, although Goffman is known for his ideas about frames and frame analysis, few people are likely to have read the whole of his rather long book. Even those who have read it will probably only remember this simple lesson: frames are important. We should not forget that humans compress information. Indeed, intelligence involves the meaningful compression of information. Only in some artificial domains is memory praised for its own sake. The great stoic thinker Senecæ criticized historians for the meaningless registration of past events (Senecæ, 2007). He describes it (Senecæ, 2007, p. 49) as "fruitless dedication to unnecessary things." Sometimes, I find it more useful to converse with the masters of the past than with today's historians who have not heeded Senecæ's lesson. The reason is that memory is about meaning, and those who neglect this have nothing to say about real life.

SUMMARY

- The chapter explores the way integrating memory into LLMs enhances their ability to analyze conversations, allowing them to maintain continuity across interactions and provide more contextually informed interpretations.
- It demonstrates how conversations evoke memories, which can be analyzed using Goffman's frame and footing theories to understand participants' roles, motivations, and relational dynamics in a deeper and more meaningful way.
- Instead of merely accumulating data, the chapter advocates for a memory system that mirrors human intelligence by retaining only meaningful information. This approach helps filter out less relevant details and focuses on what truly informs the understanding of conversations.
- I used examples from Ingmar Bergman's *Scenes from a Marriage* to illustrate how memory can provide a richer analysis of interpersonal dynamics, particularly when interpreting emotionally complex interactions between characters like Johan and Marianne.
- I also introduced the concept of *reflection* within LLMs, allowing them to improve their performance over time. By reflecting on previous analyses and adapting instructions, LLMs can offer more nuanced and sophisticated conversational models that better mimic human memory and understanding.

NOTE

1 https://www.mem0.ai/

REFERENCES

Open Science Collaboration. (2015). Estimating the reproducibility of psychological science. *Science*, 349(6251), aac4716.

Senecæ, L. (2007). *DE BREVITATE VITAE*. Israel: Nahar Books.

5

AI FOR ANALYZING SHIFTS
IN A CONVERSATION

CONVERSATIONS ARE NONLINEAR

In the preface, I explained that conversations evolve nonlinearly, which means that the progression of the conversation does not follow a simple and predictable path. Here is an example from *No Country for Old Men*.[1] This is a tantalizing movie that revolves around a deadly game of cat and mouse initiated by a failed drug deal. The story begins when Llewelyn Moss, a tough hunter and Vietnam veteran, stumbles upon the aftermath of the failed drug deal in the desert. Among the dead bodies, he finds a briefcase containing $2 million, which he decides to take. This decision sets off a chain of events marked by relentless violence, primarily driven by the menacing presence of Anton Chigurh, a hitman hired to recover the money. Chigurh is a cold, psychopathic killer who operates with a sense of twisted morality and sadistic pleasure. Throughout the film, Chigurh is depicted as a primordial force of nature—unstoppable and unfeeling, embodying the chaotic and violent world that Sheriff Ed Tom Bell feels increasingly powerless against. Chigurh's chilling approach to life and death is exemplified in a scene where he spares a gas station owner's life based on the outcome of a coin toss, a gesture that symbolizes his perspective of the world as a game of chance. Let us analyze the gas station scene.

DOI: 10.1201/9781003591047-5

In this tense scene, Chigurh (played by Javier Bardem) converses with an old gas station owner. The scene is set in a desert gas station where Chigurh is the only client. The dialogue begins innocently enough, with Chigurh asking the owner simple questions about his business. However, the conversation quickly takes a darker turn as Chigurh begins to behave in a rather threatening way. The owner starts to become visibly nervous, particularly when Chigurh flips a coin and asks him to call it, implying that the outcome will determine whether he lives or dies. The tension builds as the owner, confused and terrified, reluctantly calls the coin toss. Fortunately, he calls it correctly, and Chigurh spares his life, but the scene leaves us with a sense of dread. It evolves from an ordinary interaction to a life-or-death moment, with Chigurh's calm and calculated approach amplifying the tension. The nonlinear progression of the conversation underscores the unpredictable nature of Chigurh's character.

To understand the evolving dynamic of this conversation, I first segment it into overlapping windows of three utterances. Here is the prompt I used to segment the conversation.

PROMPT 5.1

Instructions for Analyzing a Conversation Using the Sliding Window Approach (Window of 3, Slide of 1)

Objective: To analyze a conversation by breaking it into overlapping segments (windows) of three utterances and examining each segment for ambiance, speech acts, and relational dynamics using Goffman's theory of frames and footings.

Step 1: Define the Sliding Window Parameters

Window size: Each window will include three utterances.

Slide increment: Shift the window forward by one utterance after each analysis, creating overlapping segments.

Step 2: Identify the Ambiance in Each Window

Mood and atmosphere: Determine the general mood and atmosphere within the three-utterance window. Is it tense, playful, sarcastic, affectionate, etc.?

Tone and quality: Identify the tone of the interaction—whether it's teasing, serious, lighthearted, or critical.

Character of the interaction: Recognize any underlying emotional or relational dynamics that characterize the interaction within the window.

Step 3: Identify Speech Acts in Each Window

Categorize speech acts: For each utterance in the window, identify the type of speech act being performed. Common categories include assertion, question, command, compliment, complaint, etc.

Relational dynamics: Consider how each speech act contributes to or alters the relational dynamics between the speakers.

Step 4: Analyze the Frames and Footings in Each Window

Criteria for Identifying the Frame

Topic and content: Analyze the topics introduced and the way they contextualize the conversation.

Purpose and intent: Consider the speaker's intent and the way it shapes the interaction.

Implicit assumptions: Look for underlying assumptions guiding the conversation.

Shifts in focus: Monitor any shifts in the focus of the conversation that may indicate a change in the frame.

Criteria for Identifying the Footing

Speaker's role: Identify how each speaker positions themselves within the interaction.

Tone and attitude: Analyze the tone to determine how each speaker positions themselves in relation to the content and others.

Interactional alignment: Assess how speakers align or distance themselves from others.

Use of pronouns: Pay attention to pronouns that indicate alignment or confrontation.

Responsiveness to others: Observe how speakers respond to previous statements, which may indicate shifts in footing.

Incorporate Ambiance into the Frame and Footing Analysis

Use the identified ambiance as a lens to interpret the frames and footings. Consider how the mood and atmosphere influence the roles, stances, and alignments of the participants.

Step 5: Document and Interpret the Analysis

Analyze the First Window

Begin by analyzing the first three utterances for ambiance, speech acts, and frames/footing.

Shift the Window Forward by One Utterance

Move the window forward by one utterance and repeat the analysis for the next set of three utterances.

Continue Sliding and Analyzing

Continue this process until you have analyzed all overlapping segments of the text.

Interpret the Overall Dynamics

After analyzing all windows, interpret the way the conversation evolves over time. Consider how the shifting frames, footings, and ambiance contribute to the overall interaction.

Example Structure for Each Window Analysis

Window 1: Utterances 1–3

Ambiance identification: Describe the mood, tone, and character.

Speech act identification: Identify the speech acts in each utterance.

Frame and footing analysis: Analyze the frame and footing, using ambiance as the background.

Window 2: Utterances 2–4

Ambiance identification: Describe the mood, tone, and character.

Speech act identification: Identify the speech acts in each utterance.

Frame and footing analysis: Analyze the frame and footing, using ambiance as the background.

Window 3: Utterances 3–5
> Ambiance identification: Describe the mood, tone, and character.
> Speech act identification: Identify the speech acts in each utterance.
> Frame and footing analysis: Analyze the frame and footing, using ambiance as the background.
> END

TRANSITIONS IN A CONVERSATION

The sliding window approach allows us to analyze the dynamics piece by piece and identify important transitions. Let's see what we get by analyzing the conversation between the psychopathic hitman and the gas station owner. The conversation is as follows:

Chigurh:	How much?
Owner:	Sixty-nine cents.
Chigurh:	This. And the gas.
Owner:	Y'all getting any rain up your way?
Chigurh:	What way would that be?
Owner:	I seen you was from Dallas.
Chigurh:	What business is it of yours where I'm from, friendo?
Owner:	I didn't mean nothin' by it.

The model produced the following output:

Sliding Window Analysis of the Conversation

Window 1: Utterances 1–3

Ambiance Identification
> Mood: The mood is tense, with a sense of underlying threat.
> Tone: The tone is direct and matter-of-fact, with Chigurh exhibiting a controlled demeanor.
> Character of the interaction: Chigurh's curt responses establish a power dynamic where he subtly asserts dominance.

Speech Act Identification

> Utterance 1 (Chigurh: How much?): Question—Chigurh inquires about the cost.
>
> Utterance 2 (Owner: Sixty-nine cents.): Assertion—The proprietor provides the price.
>
> Utterance 3 (Chigurh: This. And the gas.): Command—Chigurh is specifying his purchase.

Frame and Footing Analysis

> Frame: The interaction is framed around a transactional exchange, with Chigurh initiating the conversation about the price and his purchase.

Footing

> > Chigurh's role: He positions himself as the dominant figure, controlling the conversation with terse, commanding language.
> >
> > Owner's role: The proprietor is subservient, responding passively to Chigurh's questions and commands.
> >
> > Interactional alignment: Chigurh's controlled tone and direct language suggest he is testing the boundaries, while the proprietor is cautious and deferential.
> >
> > Ambiance influence: The tense mood reinforces the power imbalance, with Chigurh maintaining an air of intimidation.

Completing the analysis for the final window, we get the following:

Window 3: Utterances 3–5

Ambiance identification

> Mood: The mood becomes increasingly tense and confrontational.
>
> Tone: The tone is now more threatening, particularly in Chigurh's response.
>
> Character of the interaction: The interaction is marked by an escalating power struggle, with Chigurh asserting dominance.

Speech Act Identification

> Utterance 3 (Chigurh: This. And the gas.): Command—Chigurh emphasizes the purchase, maintaining control.

Utterance 4 (Owner: Y'all getting any rain up your way?): Question—The proprietor attempts to shift the focus to small talk.

Utterance 5 (Chigurh: What way would that be?): Question—Chigurh challenges the proprietor, implying suspicion and dominance.

Frame and Footing Analysis

Frame: The frame is now confrontational, with Chigurh challenging the proprietor's intent behind his question.

Footing

Chigurh's role: Chigurh positions himself as the aggressor, questioning the owner's motives.

Owner's role: The owner becomes defensive, retreating from his attempt at small talk.

Interactional alignment: Chigurh's question shifts the alignment from transactional to interrogative, further destabilizing the interaction.

Ambiance influence: The increasing tension in the ambiance amplifies the power struggle, with Chigurh's dominance becoming more overt.

At this point, we may want the model to detect a *change* in a conversation. Instead of designing a prompt, I asked the model to do it by itself:

PROMPT 5.2

Propose a way in which I can use the outputs of the above-proposed prompt to identify a change in the conversation.
END

The model came up with the following suggestion:

To identify changes in the conversation using the outputs of the sliding window analysis, you can follow a structured approach that compares the ambiance, speech acts, and frames/footings across the different windows. Here's a proposed method:

PROMPT 5.3

Step 1: Create a Summary Table for Each Window

Columns for Each Component

> **Ambiance**: Summarize each window's mood, tone, and character.
>
> **Speech acts**: List the types of speech acts identified in each window.
>
> **Frames**: Describe the frame established or shifted within each window.
>
> **Footing**: Note the footings of each speaker within the window.

Step 2: Identify Patterns and Trends

Track Changes in Ambiance

> Compare the ambiance across windows. Look for shifts in mood, tone, or character. For example, a change from a playful ambiance to a more sarcastic or tense ambiance may indicate a shift in the emotional undercurrent of the conversation.
>
> **Indicator of change**: A significant shift in ambiance suggests a change in the emotional or relational dynamics of the conversation.

Analyze Speech Act Dynamics

> Observe the types of speech acts used across windows. A change in the prevalence of certain speech acts (e.g., from compliments to critiques) can signal a shift in the purpose or tone of the conversation.
>
> **Indicator of change**: A shift from supportive speech acts to more confrontational ones, or the introduction of new speech acts (e.g., proposals or challenges), can indicate a change in the direction or intensity of the conversation.

Examine Shifts in Frames

Look for any changes in the frames established by the speakers. A shift in focus or context, such as moving from personal validation to relational tension, suggests a change in the overall direction of the conversation.

Indicator of change: A shift in a frame, especially if it leads to a new topic or focus, can indicate a significant change in the conversation.

Monitor Footing Adjustments

Track how the footings of the speakers evolve. Changes in the way speakers position themselves (e.g., from playful to defensive) can reveal shifts in power dynamics, relational alignments, or the tone of the conversation.

Indicator of change: A shift in footing, such as a speaker moving from a vulnerable to a dominant position, can indicate a change in the balance of power or emotional tenor of the conversation.

Step 3: Synthesize and Interpret the Changes

Compare Consecutive Windows

Compare each window with the previous one. Identify and note any significant changes in ambiance, speech acts, frames, and footings.

Example interpretation: If the ambiance shifts from playful to tense, and the speech acts move from compliments to criticisms, this suggests the conversation has moved from light banter to a more serious or confrontational phase.

Identify Key Transition Points

Look for windows where multiple components (ambiance, speech acts, frames, footings) shift simultaneously. These points often indicate critical transitions in the conversation.

Example interpretation: If both the frame and footing shift significantly between two windows, this might indicate a turning point in the conversation where the focus or power dynamics changes.

Visualize the Changes

Create a timeline or flowchart that maps out the shifts in ambiance, speech acts, frames, and footings across the windows. This visualization can help you see the overall trajectory of the conversation and pinpoint where significant changes occur.

Draw Conclusions

Based on the identified changes, summarize the key transitions in the conversation. Describe how the conversation evolved and what these changes reveal about the interaction dynamics.

Step 4: Use Changes to Inform Further Analysis

Focus on Transition Points

Conduct a deeper analysis of windows where significant changes occur. Explore why these shifts happened and what they reveal about the participants' motivations or the underlying issues.

Consider the Broader Context

Relate the changes in the conversation to the broader context of the interaction. How do these shifts align with the overall relationship dynamics, goals, or external influences on the conversation?

END

I asked the model to apply the instructions, and the model produced Table 5.1.

Step 1: Summary Table for Each Window

Here we see how the model organized the conversation according to the sliding window approach.

TABLE 5.1 Sliding Windows and Their Dimensions

WINDOW	AMBIANCE	SPEECH ACTS	FRAMES	FOOTING
Window 1	Tense, controlled, underlying threat	Question, Assertion, Command	Transactional exchange focused on purchase	Chigurh dominant, Proprietor passive
Window 2	Tense, slight discomfort with shift to small talk	Assertion, Command, Question	Shift from transactional to personal interaction	Chigurh guarded, Proprietor attempts casual shift
Window 3	Increasingly tense and confrontational	Command, Question, Question	Confrontational, challenging the proprietor's intent	Chigurh aggressive, Proprietor defensive

Step 2: Identify Patterns and Trends

Track Changes in Ambiance

Window 1 to window 2: The ambiance remains tense but with an added layer of discomfort as the conversation shifts from transactional to an attempted casual interaction.

Window 2 to window 3: The tension escalates as the conversation becomes more confrontational, with Chigurh challenging the proprietor's intent.

Indicator of change: The shift from a controlled transaction to a tense, confrontational ambiance suggests an escalation in the emotional and relational dynamics, signaling an increase in underlying conflict.

Analyze Speech Act Dynamics

Window 1 to window 2: The speech acts shift from a transactional focus (questions and commands) to include an attempt at small talk by the proprietor.

Window 2 to window 3: Chigurh's introduction of confrontational speech acts, with repeated questioning, indicates a shift toward an aggressive interrogation.

Indicator of change: The shift from transactional to confrontational speech acts suggests a change in the purpose of the conversation, moving from a simple exchange to a power struggle.

Examine Shifts in Frames

Window 1 to window 2: The frame shifts from a transactional exchange to a more personal interaction as the proprietor attempts to engage Chigurh beyond the transaction.

Window 2 to window 3: The frame shifts again to a confrontational context as Chigurh challenges the proprietor's motives.

Indicator of change: The frame shifts from transactional to personal and then to confrontational, signaling a progression in the focus and intensity of the conversation.

Monitor Footing Adjustments

Window 1 to window 2: Chigurh maintains dominance, but the proprietor attempts to shift the footing toward a more casual interaction.

Window 2 to window 3: Chigurh's footing becomes more aggressive and dominant, while the proprietor becomes defensive.

Indicator of change: The shift in footing, particularly Chigurh's move from dominance to outright aggression, indicates a change in the power dynamics, with the conversation becoming more imbalanced.

This output is detailed but may in fact be too detailed. The next step brings us closer to identifying the general trend.

Step 3: Synthesize and Interpret the Changes

Compare Consecutive Windows

Window 1 to window 2: The transition from a controlled transactional interaction to an awkward attempt at small talk introduces a subtle shift in dynamics, making the ambiance more uncomfortable.

Window 2 to window 3: The escalation from casual discomfort to direct confrontation marks a significant turning point in the conversation. Chigurh's aggressive questioning disrupts any remaining pretense of a normal exchange.

Example interpretation: The conversation evolves from a tense transaction to an uncomfortable attempt at casual interaction before escalating into a direct confrontation. The ambiance, speech acts, and footing all indicate a progression toward increasing tension and conflict.

Identify Key Transition Points

Transition Point: The shift between window 2 and window 3 is critical, where both the frame and footing shift significantly, indicating a turning point in the conversation toward open conflict.

Example interpretation: The simultaneous shift in frame and footing between windows 2 and 3 indicates a critical transition from discomfort to confrontation, driven by Chigurh's aggressive questioning.

Visualize the Changes

Timeline or flowchart: A visual representation would show the progression from transactional to personal and finally to confrontational frames, corresponding shifts in ambiance and footing, highlighting the key transition point.

Draw Conclusions

Example conclusion: "The conversation starts as a tense but controlled transaction, which becomes increasingly uncomfortable as the proprietor attempts to shift the interaction to small talk. Chigurh's aggressive response escalates the situation into a direct confrontation, revealing the underlying power struggle and tension in the interaction."

The final conclusion is what we were looking for:

It is a situation evolving into a confrontation and threat.

The next step explains how the analysis may inform further analysis.

Step 4: Use Changes to Inform Further Analysis

Focus on Transition Points

Deeper analysis: Examine why Chigurh reacts so strongly to the proprietor's small talk and how this reaction aligns with his character's need for control and dominance.

Consider the Broader Context

Broader context: Relate these shifts to Chigurh's overall persona and the tension inherent in the setting, contributing to the inevitable confrontation.

This structured approach allows for a detailed analysis of the conversation, revealing the subtle and overt shifts in dynamics that contribute to the overall interaction.

In order to explain why Chigurh behaves in this way, it would clearly be interesting to analyze the personalities of the participants in a conversation. I dedicate Chapter 7 to this task. Returning to the present exercise, I asked the model to reanalyze the whole conversation in the gas station, score the dimensions it analyzed, and visualize them. The model scored the dimensions as follows.

The scaled values in the visualization were assigned on the basis of a qualitative analysis rather than precise numerical measurements. The dimensions were represented as follows.

Ambiance (tension): Values were attributed on the basis of the perceived level of tension within each window. Higher values indicate greater tension, reflecting the rising or falling emotional stakes.

Speech acts (confrontation): Values here represent the number of direct confrontational or commanding speech acts within each window. The value increased as the confrontation or directness in the speech acts increased.

Frame shifts: The values reflect the number of significant shifts in the frame within each window. A higher value indicates more substantial changes in the context or focus of the conversation.

Footing shifts: Values were attributed on the basis of the intensity of shifts in the power dynamics or roles between the speakers. Higher values indicate more pronounced shifts in footing, such as a change from a neutral stance to an aggressive or submissive one.

This led to the visualization of the whole conversation in Figure 5.1.

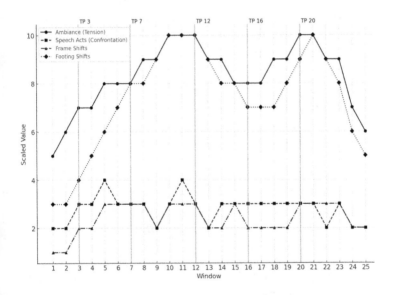

FIGURE 5.1 Visualization of the points where a change occurs in the conversation. Ambiance (tension): Solid line (-) with circle markers. Speech acts (confrontation): Dashed line (–) with square markers. Frame shifts: Dash-dot line (-.) with triangle markers. Footing shifts: Dotted line (:) with diamond markers. Transition points are highlighted with vertical gray lines, ensuring that the key moments of change are visible.

The model explained that:

> The analysis identified transition points on the basis of notable changes in the dynamics of the conversation across several dimensions: ambiance (tension), speech acts (confrontation), frames, and footing. These points are marked when a significant shift or escalation occurs in one or more of these areas. Here's how each was considered:
>
> Ambiance (tension): A transition point is marked when a mood or emotional intensity changes, such as a shift from a relatively calm exchange to a tense or menacing atmosphere.

For example, in transition point 3, the hitman responds aggressively to the gas station owner's innocent question: "What business is it of yours where I'm from, friendo?" The owner was just trying to make small talk with a client and this was met with an aggressive response in the form of a confrontational speech act. This is also a turning point as regards the speech acts. A transition point occurs when the nature of the speech acts changes, such as moving from questions to direct orders or confrontational utterances.

With respect to frames, the model explains:

> A transition point is identified when the *conversational frame shifts significantly*, such as when the discussion moves from a transactional frame to a more personal or philosophical one. This is often linked to a change in the topic or the underlying purpose of the conversation.

This happens in window 3 when the frame shifts from interpersonal to confrontational.

With respect to footings:

> Transition points are noted when there is a significant change in the way the speakers position themselves relative to each other. For instance, a shift from a neutral to a dominant stance by one speaker or a move from a cooperative to a defensive posture marks a transition.

This shift is illustrated in window 7, where Chigurh maintains control, and the owner becomes desperate to end the interaction. This is a point where Chigurh's psychopathic stance is fully exposed. He becomes the hunter, and the gas station owner becomes the prey.

TRANSITIONS IN SCENES FROM A MARRIAGE

Using the same prompts and approach, I returned to *Scenes from a Marriage* to identify the dynamics of the first scene, where Marianne and Johan are interviewed. Let's examine the first three windows:

Mrs. Palm:	"Well, let's get cracking. I generally use a standard opener to put people at ease."
Johan:	"I'm not particularly nervous."
Mrs. Palm:	"All the better. So, how would you describe yourselves in a few words?"
Johan:	"That's tricky."
Mrs. Palm:	"Is it?"

The first window has a neutral and procedural ambiance. Still, when we shift to the second window, the ambiance becomes slightly tense, and the frame shifts to self-assessment, where Johan asserts that describing himself in a few words is 'tricky,' and his stance is one of insecurity. When we shift to the third window, the model identifies Johan's assertion that it's tricky as slightly confrontational with a sarcastic undertone. After all, it is an interview for a women's magazine, and the interviewer's opening request is a 'standard opener' to 'put people at ease.' In this context, Johan's response is not cooperative. Instead of collaborating with the interviewer's 'standard opener,' he points out that her request for self-presentation is tricky. The model intelligently identifies his response as indicative of his projected self. By refusing to simply collaborate with Mrs. Palm, Johan exposes his stance. Instead of simply addressing Mrs. Palm's request, he reflects on it, framing it as tricky, complex, difficult, or deceptive. In what sense is it a tricky request? Johan later explains that by addressing her request, she might get the wrong impression that he is cocky and arrogant. However, this is the exact impression we get about Johan from his self-presentation and the way Marianne describes him. His footing, stance, or 'projected self' is that of a self-confident, extrovert, and amusing individual. An arrogant, confident, and funny guy. This is a false self, as will be revealed in the dynamics later on.

The nonlinear dynamics of a conversation can be analyzed by using the large language model (LLM) to segment the conversation into sliding windows and make an intelligent analysis of their dimensions and the changes in those dimensions as we move to the following window. The same general approach will be developed further in the next chapter, where I focus on analyzing topics and seeing how they change as the conversation unfolds.

SUMMARY

- The chapter explores how conversations often unfold nonlinearly, i.e., interactions evolve unpredictably rather than following a simple, linear progression.
- I introduced a sliding window approach to conversation analysis, segmenting dialogues into overlapping series of utterances. This method allows for a detailed analysis of transitions.
- In addition, I provide a structured methodology to identify shifts in conversation. This approach offers insights into the underlying power dynamics, evolving roles, and emotional undercurrents of the interactions.
- The gas station scene from the movie *No Country for Old Men* is used as a case study to demonstrate how conversations can shift dramatically in tone and intent. The analysis reveals how the interaction moves from a seemingly mundane exchange to a tense and confrontational encounter, highlighting the unpredictable nature of conversational dynamics.

- Finally, the chapter outlines a method for identifying transition points in conversations by tracking changes in ambiance, speech acts, frames, and footings across different segments. This method helps us to understand how and why conversations shift, providing a deeper understanding of the participants' intentions and overall trajectories.

NOTE

1 https://en.wikipedia.org/wiki/No_Country_for_Old_Men

6

SHIFTS IN TOPIC AND WHAT THEY CAN TEACH US

"DOES-HE-LOOK-LIKE-A-BITCH?!"

A topic in a conversation refers to the central subject or theme being discussed. It can be thought of as the main idea that the speakers focus on at any given moment. A topic shift occurs when the focus of a conversation changes from one subject to another. A topic shift is, therefore, *a shift in attention*, and a shift in attention is indicative of where the mind is heading. Therefore, identifying these shifts helps us to understand the dynamics of the conversation, including the participants' underlying motivations. In this chapter, I show how to prompt the model to identify topic shifts in a conversation and, from these shifts, learn something interesting about the participants and the evolving dynamics of the conversation. I start by returning to *Pulp Fiction* and analyzing another iconic scene.

In one of the tense and iconic scenes from *Pulp Fiction*, Jules (played by Samuel Jackson) and Vincent (played by John Travolta), two enforcers working for a vicious crime boss by the name of Marsellus Wallace, confront three young men who have crossed their boss. An interesting conversation evolves while they are entering the apartment where the three guys reside. At this stage in the

DOI: 10.1201/9781003591047-6

movie, we are already familiar with Jules and Vincent's conversation style. They amuse themselves with the different names a quarter-pound hamburger is called in Paris and engage in a philosophical discussion about the meaning of foot massage. Their conversations are both mundane and odd.

When entering the apartment, they encounter the three frightened young men. The conversation is led by Jules, who interrogates Brett, one of the young men, about their business with Marsellus Wallace. Jules first engages Brett in a seemingly harmless, albeit rather bizarre, dialogue about the food they're eating. He asks him about the hamburger he is eating for breakfast, tastes it, and sips some of his Sprite. His approach combines an exaggerated form of politeness with a threatening approach that is disrespectful of personal boundaries. Shoving your hands into a stranger's plate of food is disrespectful and signals that a boundary has been crossed.

As the conversation progresses, the tone shifts dramatically. Jules abruptly shoots one of the young men, Roger, mid-sentence, shocking Brett and asserting control. He continues to intimidate Brett, demanding a description of Marsellus Wallace and becoming increasingly aggressive when Brett hesitates to describe Marsellus as black. When Brett inadvertently responds with "What?" Jules loses patience and shoots Brett in the shoulder, further terrorizing him. An interesting shift occurs at the turning point from talking about the food the guys are eating to the question about Marcellus:

Jules:	Does-he-look-like-a-bitch?!
Brett:	No.
Jules:	Then why did you try to fuck 'im like a bitch?!

It is easy to spot the shift in topic, but it is not just a topic shift: it is an event telling us something deeper about the conversation, the participants, and the dynamics.

THE LLM CAN IDENTIFY
SHIFTS IN TOPIC

To gain a deeper understanding of this interaction, I used the following prompt.

PROMPT 6.1

I am interested in identifying topic shifts in a conversation. Propose a prompt that can identify (1) topic shifts in a conversation and (2) the source of each topic shift.

Changes of topic can occur in a conversation for various reasons. Understanding these shifts requires us to examine the content of the conversation and the participants' underlying cognitive processes. Here are some key aspects:

1. Cognitive associations: Participants often change topic as a result of associative thinking. If a word or concept in the current topic reminds a participant of another topic, they might introduce this new topic into the conversation. This is often an unconscious process in which the mind connects related ideas.

2. Contextual triggers: External factors like the environment, new information, or the presence of other people can trigger a topic shift. For example, if someone joins a conversation, their presence might prompt a new topic related to their interests or expertise.

3. Social dynamics: The dynamics between participants, such as power relations, attention, and the desire to connect or disagree, can also drive shifts. For instance, if someone feels their point of view isn't being heard, they might change the topic to regain control or shift the conversation to a topic where they feel more confident.

4. Purposeful redirection: Sometimes, participants intentionally shift the topic to steer the conversation toward a particular goal. This might happen in professional settings,

debates, or negotiations, where controlling the topic can influence the outcome.

5. Fatigue or disinterest: If participants lose interest in the current topic or feel it has been exhausted, they might introduce a new topic to maintain engagement. This can also happen when participants sense that others are losing interest and shift the conversation to keep it lively.

6. Cultural norms and expectations: Different cultures have varying norms about how and when to change topics. In some cultures, abrupt shifts might be seen as rude, while in others, they might be a natural part of the conversation flow.

END

The model proposed the following prompt.

PROMPT 6.2

Prompt for Identifying Topic Shifts and Their Sources in a Conversation

1. Identifying Topic Shifts
   Review the conversation text and divide it into segments based on changes in the main subject or focus of discussion.

   Highlight where the conversation moves from one topic to another, noting subtle and abrupt shifts. Pay attention to changes in key terms, the introduction of new ideas, and shifts in the participants' focus.

2. Determining the Source of Each Topic Shift
   Cognitive associations: Identify whether the shift occurs because a word or concept in the previous topic reminded a participant of another idea. A participant often indicates this by linking the new topic to something just mentioned.

   Contextual triggers: Look for external factors like a change in the environment, the introduction of new information, or a new participant joining the conversation. Note whether the shift occurs shortly after these changes.

Social dynamics: Analyze whether the shift is driven by changes in the social dynamics, such as a participant trying to regain control, assert dominance, or steer the conversation toward a topic where they feel more confident.

Purposeful redirection: Identify whether the shift appears to be intentional to steer the conversation toward a specific goal or agenda. This is often seen in professional or strategic contexts.

Fatigue or disinterest: Observe whether the shift occurs after a prolonged discussion on a single topic, indicating possible fatigue or loss of interest. Note whether the new topic is introduced to re-engage the participants.

Cultural norms and expectations: Consider whether cultural norms might have influenced the timing and manner of the shift. If the conversation occurs across cultures, note any differences in how and when topics change.

3. Additional Considerations

Frequency of shifts: Track how often topics shift and whether these shifts follow a predictable pattern (e.g., after a certain number of exchanges or when a particular participant speaks).

Participant roles: Note which participants are most likely to initiate shifts and whether certain individuals consistently bring the conversation back to previous topics or push it forward.

END

I then gave the model the following instruction:

Propose how to improve the prompt

The model suggested this:

To improve the prompt, we can add more specificity to the instructions, offer examples for clarity, and introduce analytical techniques or tools that can be used to systematically identify and categorize topic shifts. Here's an enhanced version:

Enhanced Prompt for Identifying Topic Shifts and Their Sources in a Conversation

1. Identifying Topic Shifts
   Segmentation: Begin by reading the conversation and breaking it into smaller segments, ideally by sentence or speaker turn. Look for transitions where the main subject or focus changes.
   Indicators of shifts: Pay attention to explicit indicators such as phrases ("Speaking of…," "That reminds me of…"), the introduction of new concepts, or shifts in the use of key terms.
   Subtle vs. abrupt shifts: Distinguish between subtle shifts, where the topic gradually evolves, and abrupt shifts, where the change is more sudden. Highlight or annotate these shifts in the text.
   Tools: Utilize text analysis tools (e.g., topic modeling, keyword frequency analysis) to identify objectively where shifts occur.
2. Determining the Source of Each Topic Shift
   Cognitive Associations
   Description: A shift driven by associative thinking, where a participant connects a word or idea in the current topic to a different topic.
   Example: If the conversation is about travel and suddenly shifts to food because someone mentions a favorite dish they ate while traveling.
   Analysis: Use semantic similarity tools to trace the cognitive path that may have led to the shift.
   Contextual Triggers
   Description: A shift caused by external factors like new information, environmental changes, or new participants.

Example: A conversation about work shifts to one about personal life when someone's phone rings with a call from home.

Analysis: Note any external interruptions or changes just before the shift. Contextual data (e.g., time, location) can also be considered.

Social Dynamics

Description: A shift motivated by interpersonal dynamics, such as power struggles, attention-seeking, or the desire to connect.

Example: A participant changes the topic to something they are knowledgeable about to dominate the conversation.

Analysis: Observe non-verbal cues or changes in tone, and consider the roles of the various participants (e.g., who tends to lead or follow).

Purposeful Redirection

Description: A deliberate attempt to change the topic for strategic reasons.

Example: In a meeting, someone redirects the conversation from a controversial topic to a safer one to avoid conflict.

Analysis: Look for premeditated shifts, often following a pause or after someone gains the floor.

Fatigue or Disinterest

Description: A shift caused by the participants' waning interest in the current topic.

Example: A prolonged discussion on a technical topic is redirected to a lighter, more engaging subject.

Analysis: Monitor the duration of each topic before shifts, noting signs of fatigue like shorter responses or disengagement.

Cultural Norms and Expectations

Description: Shifts influenced by cultural expectations about conversation flow.

Example: In some cultures, participants may avoid prolonged focus on one topic, leading to frequent shifts.

Analysis: If the conversation is cross-cultural, consider cultural communication styles, norms, and practices that may influence shifts.

3. Additional Considerations

Frequency and Pattern of Shifts

Track the frequency of topic shifts throughout the conversation. Are shifts happening at regular intervals, or are they more sporadic?

Pattern analysis: Use statistical methods to analyze the timing and distribution of shifts, possibly correlating with participant roles or external factors.

Role of Participants

Identify which participants are most likely to initiate shifts and categorize them by source. Are some participants more prone to certain types of shifts (e.g., cognitive, social)?

Influence mapping: Create a map showing which participants influence the conversation flow and how often they introduce new topics.

4. Refinement and Feedback

Iterative review: After identifying and categorizing shifts, review the findings to ensure consistency. Consider whether shifts are appropriately categorized and whether there are patterns in the sources of shifts.

Feedback loop: Use feedback from other analysts or participants to refine the analysis. Are there alternative explanations for some shifts? Does the categorization align with participants' perceptions?

I asked the model to apply the improved prompt to the conversation from *Pulp Fiction*, and the model provided the analysis below.

Analysis of Topic Shifts and Their Sources in the Conversation

Segmentation and Identification of Topic Shifts

Initial greeting and interrogation: The conversation begins with Jules greeting the young men and quickly shifts to an interrogation about their relationship with Marsellus Wallace. This is an abrupt shift from a casual greeting to a tense interrogation.

The model correctly identified two different frames: greeting and interrogation.

Discussion of hamburgers: Jules steers the conversation to the seemingly trivial topic of hamburgers, questioning Brett about his meal. This subtle shift creates a false sense of security and disarms the young men.

Discussing hamburgers is a bizarre shift in the conversation. It emphasizes how Jules allows himself to create incoherence in the conversation, disrespecting the maxim of mutual communication and understanding. Coherence and incoherence will be discussed in Chapter 8, as they point to the 'logical' aspect of the conversation and indicate other interesting dimensions, such as power relations.

The briefcase: The topic shifts again when Jules directs Roger to reveal the location of the hidden briefcase, returning to the original purpose of their visit. This is a purposeful redirection to the main agenda.

Brett's apology: After Vincent retrieves the briefcase, Brett attempts to apologize and explain the situation, marking a shift toward a more defensive and desperate tone.

Interrogation about Marsellus Wallace: Jules abruptly changes the topic to an intense interrogation about Marsellus Wallace, challenging Brett to describe him. This marks another abrupt shift, escalating the tension.

The model correctly mapped the shifts, and here we get to the more interesting point: determining the source of each change of topic.

Determining the Source of Each Topic Shift

Cognitive associations: The shift from interrogation to discussing hamburgers is driven by Jules' associative thinking, linking the breakfast to the current tense situation to disarm Brett momentarily.

The model suggests that the shift results from association. However, this allegedly association-based shift is functional. Allowing himself to go astray from the main issue of the conversation, Jules communicates his full control of the situation. The model identifies other sources as well.

Purposeful redirection: The conversation returns to the briefcase under the bed, a deliberate attempt by Jules to refocus on their mission after distracting Brett with casual talk.

Social dynamics: The conversation shifts reflect Jules' control over the situation. He dominates the interaction, shifting topics strategically to maintain his psychological upper hand.

Fatigue or disinterest: Brett's failed attempt to explain himself and de-escalate the situation is met with Jules shifting back to an interrogation, indicating Jules' disinterest in Brett's justifications.

Cultural norms and expectations: Jules' mockery of Brett's intelligence (e.g., discussing the metric system) subtly shifts the conversation to reinforce cultural and intellectual dominance, a common trope in power dynamics.

Additional Considerations

Frequency and pattern of shifts: Jules frequently shifts topics, keeping Brett off balance and ensuring he remains in control. The shifts are both abrupt and calculated, creating a pattern of dominance.

Role of participants: Jules initiates all the topic shifts, demonstrating his role as the dominant figure in the conversation. Brett and the others react passively, highlighting the power imbalance.

The last output of the model is the most interesting:

> The conversation shifts are consistently categorized as Jules' strategic maneuvers to maintain control. The pattern of shifts aligns with Jules' intentions to intimidate and assert dominance.

> A review of the analysis would likely confirm that the shifts disorient the young men, preventing them from mounting any defense or escape, reinforcing the categorization of shifts as deliberate and power-driven.

We can see that the model analyzed the topic shifts in a way that validly exposed the underlying dynamics. The model interprets the shifts as Jules' *attempt to control, intimidate, and assert dominance*. This is the bottom line of the analysis. The shifts are indicative of the conversation dynamics. I further asked the model to elaborate on these conclusions, and its further remarks deepen our understanding.

WHAT CAN WE LEARN FROM TOPIC SHIFTS?

I asked the model:

> What can we learn from the topic shifts about the participants and the conversation dynamics? Explain how a topic shift can inform us about the participants and the dynamics.

The model provided the following answer:

> From the topic shifts in this conversation, we can infer several key insights about the participants and the dynamics of their interaction:

> 1. **Jules' Dominance and Control**
>   Topic shift to hamburgers: When Jules shifts the conversation from a serious interrogation to a discussion about hamburgers, it's a strategic move to disarm Brett and make

him feel momentarily at ease. This shift highlights Jules'
control over the conversation and his ability to manipulate
the situation. It shows that Jules is physically dominant
and psychologically in charge, using seemingly trivial
topics to assert his authority and unsettle the young men.

We have already recognized the first lesson: Jules' dominance and control. However, the next point adds another
layer of understanding.

2. **Brett's Vulnerability**

Response to the metric system discussion: When Jules shifts
the topic to a discussion about the metric system, Brett's
compliance and attempt to answer ("Because of the metric system?") reveal his vulnerability and desperation to
appease Jules. This shift and Brett's reaction indicate his
recognition of the power dynamics and his fear of escalating the situation. Brett's willingness to engage in trivial
banter underscores his anxiety and submissive position.

Brett's vulnerability is used and manipulated through Jules'
associative moves.

3. **Use of Cognitive Associations to Disarm**

Associating food with threat: Jules' transition from discussing the hamburger to questioning Brett about Marsellus
Wallace uses cognitive associations to juxtapose the casual
with the threatening. This shift indicates Jules' methodical
and manipulative nature, as he blends the ordinary (food)
with the ominous (interrogation), heightening the tension. It reflects his ability to control the narrative and keep
the young men off-balance.

This is a highly important point and what I consider
to be the most significant insight provided by the model.
Jules is not just a muscle man but a sophisticated, intelligent, and manipulative person. His shift from discussing
the taste of hamburgers to interrogations, threats, and
violence is indicative of the person and the methodology
he uses to terrorize others.

4. **Reassertion of Purpose and Authority**

   Return to the briefcase: The shift back to the briefcase under the bed after discussing hamburgers is a purposeful redirection to the main agenda, reinforcing Jules' authority. This shift reveals that, while Jules may entertain diversions, he remains focused on the objective, demonstrating his professionalism and ruthlessness. The shift back to the primary task underscores the transactional nature of the encounter—Jules is there for a specific reason, and distractions are merely tools to achieve his goal.

   This point strengthens our understanding of Jules and the dynamics of the conversation. While focused on his mission, Jules allows himself to shift topics to 'play' with his victims as a cat plays with his prey. Through these moves, Jules is exposed as a psychopath.

5. **Psychological Intimidation**

   Abrupt shift to the question about Marsellus Wallace: When Jules suddenly shifts the conversation to aggressively questioning Brett about Marsellus Wallace, it is a psychological tactic to intimidate and dominate. This shift indicates the power imbalance in the conversation, with Jules using aggressive questioning to instill fear and assert his dominance. Brett's fearful and confused responses show how the abrupt shift breaks down his composure, leaving him more vulnerable to Jules' control.

6. **Revealing Social Dynamics Through Interaction**

   Silencing Marvin and focusing on Brett: When Marvin tries to speak, and Jules immediately shuts him down, the shift back to Brett reveals the social dynamics at play. Jules' decision to ignore Marvin and focus on Brett suggests that Jules has identified Brett as the target of his intimidation, likely because Brett is seen as the leader or spokesperson. This dynamic reveals Jules' strategic thinking—he isolates and pressures the most prominent member to break the group's resistance.

7. **Escalation of Threat**

   Shift to physical violence: The final shift, where Jules transitions from verbal intimidation to shooting Roger, marks an escalation in the threat level. This shift is indicative of Jules' willingness to use violence to achieve his ends and serves as a warning to Brett. The dynamic here shows that the conversation has reached a critical point where words are no longer enough to convey the message—physical actions reinforce Jules' dominance and control.

Analyzing the shifts, we now get to the model's conclusions (my emphasis):

> The topic shifts in this conversation are *not random;* they are *deliberate* moves by Jules to maintain *control, manipulate* the young men, and achieve his objectives. Each shift reveals the participants' roles, vulnerabilities, and strategies. Jules' ability to dictate the flow of the conversation and use shifts to disorient and dominate his counterparts demonstrates his authority and the power dynamics at play. Brett's responses to these shifts highlight his fear, confusion, and eventual breakdown under pressure.

These conclusions give us a deep understanding of the conversation, the participants, and the dynamics.

IMPROVING THE MODEL

We can gain a more detailed analysis by using the following prompt.

PROMPT 6.3

Prompt for Identifying Topic Shifts and Their Sources in a Conversation

Introduction

A topic shift occurs when the focus of a conversation changes from one subject to another. Identifying these shifts helps us to understand the conversation dynamics, including the participants' underlying motivations.

Instructions

Task 1: Segment the Conversation

1.1 Divide the conversation: Break down the conversation into segments based on changes in the main subject or focus.

1.2 Categorize shifts: Label each segment as either a 'Major shift' (significant change in the central theme) or a 'Minor shift' (a small detour or tangential change).

1.3 Annotate shifts: Highlight or mark where each shift occurs in the conversation.

Task 2: Identify Indicators of Shifts

2.1 Explicit indicators: Look for explicit signals of shifts, such as phrases like "Speaking of...," "That reminds me of...," or similar transitions.

2.2 Subtle indicators: Identify more subtle changes in key terms, tone, or the introduction of new ideas that suggest a shift.

2.3 Link to segments: Connect these indicators to the segments identified in Task 1, ensuring that each shift is clearly tied to a specific part of the conversation.

Task 3: Determine the Source of Each Topic Shift

3.1 Cognitive associations: Identify whether the shift is driven by associative thinking, where a participant connects a word or idea from the current topic to a different one.

3.2 Contextual triggers: Determine whether external factors, such as new information or environmental changes, triggered the shift.

3.3 Social dynamics: Analyze whether the shift is motivated by interpersonal dynamics, such as power struggles, attention-seeking, or the desire to connect or compete.

3.4 Purposeful redirection: Check whether the shift is a deliberate attempt to change the topic for strategic reasons, perhaps to steer the conversation toward a specific goal.

3.5 Fatigue or disinterest: Assess whether the shift is due to waning interest in the current topic or a desire to keep the conversation engaging.

3.6 Cultural norms and expectations: Consider whether the shift is influenced by cultural norms regarding conversation flow, especially in cross-cultural interactions.

Task 4: Analyze the Frequency and Patterns of the Shifts

4.1 Track shifts: Record the frequency and timing of the shifts identified in Task 1.

4.2 Pattern analysis: Analyze the patterns of shifts, correlating them with participant roles, social dynamics, or external factors identified in Task 3.

Task 5: Map Participant Roles in Initiating Shifts

5.1 Identify initiators: Determine which participants are most likely to initiate shifts and link them to the sources identified in Task 3.

5.2 Create an influence map: Develop a visual or conceptual map showing which participants influence the flow of conversation, how often they introduce new topics, and how others respond.

Task 6: Reflect and Refine

6.1 Review findings: Reflect on the consistency and accuracy of the shifts and their sources when identified.

6.2 Refine analysis: Make adjustments based on any discrepancies or patterns observed during the review.

6.3 Incorporate context: Consider the broader context of the conversation, including prior interactions, relationships between participants, and the situational setting, to refine the analysis further.

The prompt results in the following output.

Task 1: Segment the Conversation

1.1 Divide the Conversation

Segment 1: Initial Greeting and Interrogation

   Focus: Jules and Vincent enter and greet the young men, initiating the conversation with an interrogation about their association with Marsellus Wallace.

   Main subject: Establishing who the young men are and their relationship to Marsellus Wallace.

Segment 2: Discussion about Hamburgers

   Focus: Jules shifts the conversation to discussing the hamburgers that Brett is eating, moving away from the interrogation.

   Main subject: The type of hamburger Brett is eating and their origin.

Segment 3: Return to the Interrogation and Briefcase Retrieval

   Focus: Jules refocuses the conversation on finding the briefcase after a brief detour on hamburgers.

   Main subject: Locating and retrieving the briefcase under the bed.

Segment 4: Brett's Attempt to Explain and Apologize

   Focus: Brett tries to explain and apologize for the situation with Marsellus Wallace.

   Main subject: Brett's explanation and attempt to de-escalate the situation.

Segment 5: Intense Interrogation about Marsellus Wallace

   Focus: Jules aggressively questions Brett about Marsellus Wallace's appearance, leading to a physical confrontation.

   Main subject: Jules' aggressive questioning and the subsequent shooting of Brett.

1.2 Categorize Shifts

Major shift: From segment 1 (interrogation) to segment 2 (discussion about hamburgers).

Minor shift: Within segment 2 (specific focus on the origin of the hamburgers).

Major shift: From segment 2 (discussion about hamburgers) to segment 3 (return to the interrogation and briefcase retrieval).

Major shift: From segment 3 (briefcase retrieval) to segment 4 (Brett's attempt to explain and apologize).

Major shift: From segment 4 (explanation) to segment 5 (aggressive interrogation about Marsellus Wallace).

1.3 Annotate Shifts

Shift 1: Jules shifts from questioning Brett to casually discussing the hamburgers.

Shift 2: The conversation subtly shifts from the general hamburger discussion to specifically asking about the origin of the hamburgers.

Shift 3: Jules returns to his main purpose, retrieving the briefcase and returning the focus to the original interrogation.

Shift 4: Brett attempts to shift the conversation toward an apology and explanation to defuse the situation.

Shift 5: Jules shifts to an intense interrogation about Marsellus Wallace, escalating the situation.

Task 2: Identify Indicators of Shifts

2.1 Explicit Indicators

Shift 1 (major): "What'cha eatin'?" Jules explicitly redirects the conversation to a casual topic (hamburgers).

Shift 3 (major): "You, Flock of Seagulls, you know what we're here for?" Jules returns explicitly to the business at hand, shifting back to the interrogation.

2.2 Subtle Indicators

Shift 2 (minor): The introduction of specific fast-food chains (McDonald's, Wendy's, Jack-in-the-Box) subtly refines the focus of the conversation within the hamburger discussion.

Shift 4 (major): Brett's apology begins with "Look, what's your name?" indicating his attempt to shift the topic to an explanation.

2.3 Link to Segments

Segment 1 to segment 2: Linked by the explicit indicator of Jules' casual question about breakfast.

Segment 2 to segment 3: Linked by Jules' direct return to the business of finding the briefcase.

Segment 3 to segment 4: Brett's attempt to explain introduces this shift.

Segment 4 to segment 5: The intensity of Jules' questioning about Marsellus Wallace signals this shift.

Task 3: Determine the Source of Each Topic Shift

3.1 Cognitive Associations

Shift 1: Jules uses associative thinking by moving from interrogation to hamburgers, using the breakfast scene to ease into a conversation and catch Brett off-guard.

3.2 Contextual Triggers

Shift 3: The sight of the briefcase under the bed triggers Jules to refocus on retrieving it, signaling a return to the main objective.

3.3 Social Dynamics

Shift 4: Brett's attempt to explain and apologize is motivated by the social dynamic of fear and a desire to de-escalate the situation.

3.4 Purposeful Redirection

Shift 5: Jules purposefully redirects the conversation back to Marsellus Wallace's appearance to assert dominance and intimidate Brett.

3.5 Fatigue or Disinterest

Shift 2: The slight shift to specific fast-food chains may reflect Jules' disinterest in the broader hamburger conversation, narrowing the focus.

3.6 Cultural Norms and Expectations

Shift 1: The casual discussion of food could reflect American cultural norms, where food conversations are a common way to establish a connection before more serious matters are discussed.

Task 4: Analyze the Frequency and Patterns of the Shifts

4.1 Track Shifts

Frequency: There are five notable shifts in the conversation, with a mix of subtle and explicit changes.

Timing: The shifts occur relatively quickly, with significant shifts often marking changes in the power dynamic or the escalation of tension.

4.2 Pattern Analysis

Pattern: The conversation alternates between casual banter and intense interrogation, creating a pattern of undermining resistance followed by aggression. This pattern correlates with Jules' role as the dominant enforcer, using shifts to manipulate the young men.

Task 5: Map Participant Roles in Initiating Shifts

5.1 Identify Initiators

Jules: Initiates most of the shifts, demonstrating his control over the conversation.

Brett: Attempts one shift (apology) but is overpowered by Jules' subsequent shifts back to aggression.

5.2 Create Influence Map

Jules: Dominates the flow of the conversation, dictating when and how shifts occur.

Brett: Reacts to shifts, only attempting to influence the conversation once, but is quickly overpowered.

Task 6: Reflect and Refine

6.1 Review Findings

Consistency: The shifts and their sources are consistently linked to Jules' strategic manipulation and Brett's reactions. Jules' control over the conversation is evident in the frequency and nature of the shifts.

6.2 Refine Analysis

Adjustment: The pattern of shifts suggests that Jules uses casual topics as a deliberate strategy to unsettle the young men before escalating to more serious threats.

The last point is the most important insight gained from the detailed analysis. Jules uses casual topics as a deliberate strategy. The model's detailed analysis has taught us that casual topics can be used as a deliberate manipulation strategy.

6.3 Incorporate Context

Broader context: Considering Jules and Vincent's roles as enforcers for Marsellus Wallace, the shifts reflect a power dynamic in which Jules uses casual conversation to mask the underlying threat, only revealing his true intentions when it serves his purpose.

The model finally concludes that:

The dynamic of the conversation is characterized by frequent topic shifts, driven primarily by Jules' manipulation. These shifts reflect Jules' strategic use of casual banter to disarm the young men, followed by abrupt returns to the central themes of intimidation and interrogation. Brett's minimal influence on the conversation highlights the power imbalance, with Jules dictating the flow and direction of the exchange. The pattern of shifts underscores the methodical and controlled nature of Jules' approach, using each shift to reinforce his dominance and maintain psychological control over the situation.

Again, the most important point is Jules' *use of shifts as a form of manipulation*. I asked the model to use the results of the recent analysis to answer the following question:

> What can we learn from the topic shifts about the participants and the dynamics of the conversation? Explain how a topic shift can inform us about the participant and the dynamics.

The model responded as follows:

> Based on the recent analysis of the conversation using the structured prompt, here's what we can learn from the topic shifts about the participants and the conversation dynamics.
>
> 1. **Jules' Strategic Control and Manipulation**
>   Shift to hamburgers (shift 1): Jules' decision to move the conversation from an interrogation about Marsellus Wallace to a casual discussion about hamburgers is a deliberate tactic. This shift indicates Jules' ability to control the flow of the conversation. By disarming Brett with a seemingly trivial topic, Jules exerts psychological control, making Brett more vulnerable when the conversation inevitably returns to the main issue. This shift shows Jules' strategic use of conversational diversions to maintain dominance.
>
> 2. **Power Dynamics and Social Roles**
>   Shift back to the briefcase (shift 3): After the brief detour into casual food talk, the return of the conversation to the briefcase under the bed reflects the underlying power dynamics. Jules quickly refocuses the conversation on the task, signaling that the earlier casual shift was only a temporary and controlled diversion. This shift highlights Jules' role as the dominant figure who dictates the terms and direction of the conversation, reinforcing his authority over the young men.
>
> 3. **Brett's Attempt to Regain Control**
>   Shift to apology (shift 4): Brett's attempt to shift the conversation toward an apology clearly indicates his desperation and recognition of the power imbalance. This shift reveals

Brett's attempt to regain some control or at least mitigate the situation, but it is quickly overridden by Jules, who redirects the conversation back to interrogation. Brett's failed shift demonstrates his lack of influence and the futility of trying to change the course set by Jules.

4. **Jules' Use of Cognitive Associations**

Shift to discussing the metric system (shift 2): When Jules shifts the conversation to the metric system and the name of a burger in France, he uses cognitive associations to blend casual banter with underlying intimidation. This shift indicates Jules' methodical approach—by discussing something seemingly irrelevant, he disarms Brett while subtly asserting his intellectual dominance. It shows how Jules uses associative thinking to control the conversation in a way that confuses and disorients the young men.

5. **Escalation of Threat and Intimidation**

Shift to aggressive interrogation (shift 5): The final major shift, where Jules intensifies the interrogation about Marsellus Wallace and confronts Brett physically, marks a clear escalation in the threat level. This shift is indicative of Jules' intent to break Brett down psychologically before resorting to violence. The abrupt nature of this shift from conversational banter to life-threatening interrogation underscores the volatile and dangerous nature of Jules' character, and it reinforces the severe power imbalance in the interaction.

The model concludes:

The topic shifts in this conversation are largely driven by Jules, who uses them to assert his dominance, manipulate the young men, and maintain control over the situation. Each shift reflects a deliberate strategy, whether it's to disarm, intimidate, or escalate the threat. Brett's attempt to shift the conversation shows his desperation but ultimately highlights his powerlessness in the face of Jules' control. The shifts reveal a dynamic where

Jules is the clear authority, using every change in topic to further his psychological manipulation, while the young men are increasingly cornered and disempowered. These dynamics illustrate how conversational control can be used as a tool for intimidation and dominance, with each shift reinforcing the enforcer's authority and the victim's vulnerability.

To understand the conversation, we don't need all the detailed analysis previously presented. We can just refer to the final conclusions of the model, which provide a valid and insightful analysis of the conversation.

When participating in a conversation, specifically if it is a stressful situation, it is extremely difficult to gain *situation awareness* and understand what is happening. Poor Brett was probably unaware of Jules' manipulations but experienced them painfully from an unreflective stance. Imagine a system observing such a conversation while providing one of the participants with situation awareness and recommendations on improving his moves. In the context of the above scene, the LLM could have informed Brett that he is dealing with a psychopath, spiraling him into fear and despair. Would it have been helpful for poor Brett? In the above scene, probably not, but in other cases, the model might be able to give us some useful directions on how to deal with such a persona and improve our stance.

SUMMARY

- Topic shifts in conversation signal the participants' *shifting attention*. This shifting attention can be detected automatically and used to enrich our understanding.
- The LLM-based analysis reveals that many topic shifts are driven by social dynamics, such as power struggles and the desire to control the conversation. Understanding these sources is crucial for uncovering the underlying motivations of the participants.

- Intentional shifts, like those seen in Jules' manipulation of the conversation, are used to disarm, intimidate, or reassert control. These shifts can be seen as purposeful redirections that reflect the psychological tactics at play, particularly in maintaining dominance over less powerful participants.
- The chapter emphasizes the importance of *recognizing patterns in topic shifts*, such as alternating between casual banter and intense interrogation. These patterns indicate the power dynamics between participants, with shifts often marking changes in control, focus, and the emotional tone of the interaction.
- The analysis shows that understanding topic shifts is key to grasping the deeper conversational dynamics, especially in scenarios where power is contested. By mapping these shifts and their sources, one can better interpret the participants' roles and strategies, and the overall trajectory of the conversation.

7

AI FOR UNDERSTANDING
INTERLOCUTORS

WHO TALKS?

The artificial boundaries and politics of the humanities result in a fragmented approach to knowledge and an arrogant distance from real-world behavior. For example, it is common practice to read papers analyzing human conversations from a linguistic or discursive perspective. You might think they have forgotten that real people have relatively coherent thoughts, emotions, and behavior patterns, which are what psychologists call 'personality.' Along the same lines, researchers studying personality usually ignore the fact that personalities are formed in a social-discursive context, where the presentation of self, to use Goffman's phrase, plays an important social function. Understanding real humans with their full complexity is possible only if we transcend the artificial boundaries laid down in academia. Large language models (LLMs) can help us to address this challenge.

Personality is important in understanding a conversation because it frames our understanding through the patterns characterizing the participants. This is another layer we should consider when analyzing conversations because it may provide us with additional background knowledge to understand the dynamics and the moves made by the participants. LLMs can serve as powerful agents for identifying the participants' personalities in a conversation (Neuman & Cohen, 2024), and the magic sauce for using their capability is to prompt them appropriately. I return to *Scenes from a Marriage* to introduce, explain, and illustrate how to understand the participants.

I analyze the opening scene, where the journalist interviews Johan and Marianne, presenting the image of an ideal and perfect couple. First, I exploit the ability of LLMs to use *external resources*. I directed the model to a paper presenting one of the most popular approaches to the clinical diagnosis of personality (Westen et al., 2012) that underlies the Shedler–Westen assessment procedure (SWAP). Although I previously criticized psychology as a science, I do find great inspiration in certain psychological ideas that we may use here to frame and inform our analysis. The following approach illustrates how we may improve the performance of the LLM by directing it to external sources of knowledge. Hence, I directed the model to the paper and asked it to read through it. I then used the following prompt.

PROMPT 7.1

Use the above taxonomy and SWAP to analyze the personality of each participant in the following conversation.

Produce a detailed personality analysis of each participant and justify your analysis through evidence from the utterances.

END

The model generated the following diagnosis:

To analyze the personality styles of each participant in this conversation using the SWAP taxonomy, I will identify specific traits and patterns of behavior in their utterances. I'll focus on how these traits align with the SWAP personality styles and provide a detailed analysis of each participant: Mrs. Palm, Johan, and Marianne.

Mrs. Palm

Personality Analysis

Obsessional personality style: Mrs. Palm exhibits traits associated with an obsessional personality style. She demonstrates a structured, methodical approach to the interview, suggesting a preference for control and order. Her interruptions to maintain the flow of the conversation and direct the participants' responses (e.g., "Let's move on to the particulars," "Maybe we should talk about your professions") indicate a need to adhere to a specific plan or procedure.

Control and critical nature: Mrs. Palm's desire to maintain control is also evident in her abrupt redirections ("Maybe we should skip that question," "Hold that pose. Look into the camera"). This indicates a potential discomfort with deviation from her intended direction, aligning with the need for order and rigid adherence to rules of the obsessional personality.

Detached and emotionally constricted: Mrs. Palm's interactions are professional and detached. She avoids emotional engagement, as seen in her response to Johan's detailed self-description and the personal nature of his remarks. This emotional constriction and focus on the task rather than the participants' emotional states align with an obsessional personality style.

Justification: Her focus on structure, control, and order, coupled with a lack of emotional engagement, suggests a personality style that is intellectualized, emotionally constricted, and critical, all of which are key traits of the obsessional personality style.

Johan

Personality Analysis

Narcissistic personality style: Johan's self-description is grandiose and self-centered. He describes himself with positive attributes such as "bright, youthful, successful, and sexy" and emphasizes his achievements and qualities, such as being a good father, son, and friend. His statement, "I might give the wrong impression," followed by detailed self-praise, reflects his awareness of his perception and desire to maintain a certain image.

- **Grandiosity and entitlement:** Johan's statements, particularly "I'm 42, but it doesn't show," and his declaration of being a "fantastic lover," exhibit classic signs of grandiosity. He presents himself as exceptional and entitled to admiration, a characteristic of the narcissistic personality style.

- **Dismissive and critical of others:** Johan's interactions with Marianne show a dismissive attitude. For instance, when he interrupts Marianne ("You said that already"), it suggests a lack of empathy and a tendency to diminish others' contributions. This behavior is typical of narcissistic individuals, who often struggle with seeing others as equals and may be dismissive of others' feelings or opinions.

- **Masking vulnerability:** Despite his confident exterior, Johan's exaggerated self-praise may mask underlying insecurities, a common trait in narcissistic personalities. His need to reaffirm his status through grand statements may be a defense against deeper feelings of inadequacy.

- **Justification:** Johan's grandiosity, entitlement, and critical attitude towards others, coupled with a possible underlying vulnerability, align with the narcissistic personality style as described in the SWAP taxonomy.

Marianne

Personality Analysis

- **Dependent-victimized personality style:** Marianne's responses throughout the conversation reflect traits of a dependent-victimized personality style. She expresses a lack of confidence ("I lack Johan's boundless self-assurance") and seems to define herself in relation to Johan rather than as an individual ("I'm married to Johan, and we have two daughters"). This suggests a dependency on Johan for her identity and self-worth.

Fear of rejection and passivity: Marianne's statements reflect a passive and unassertive demeanor. For instance, when she says, "What else should I say? This is difficult," and "I'm trying to take this seriously," it suggests a struggle with self-expression and a fear of saying the wrong thing. Her hesitation and uncertainty point to a fear of rejection or disapproval, which is characteristic of the dependent-victimized style.

Ingratiating and submissive: The way Marianne compliments Johan ("I think Johan is very nice") and her frequent deference to him ("I'll leave that to Johan") indicate an ingratiating behavior, typical of someone who is submissive and seeks approval from others, especially from those they are dependent on. Her struggle to assert her own identity or opinions further highlights this dependency.

Justification: Marianne's passive, self-doubting behavior, her dependence on Johan for validation, and her fear of rejection align with the dependent-victimized personality style as described in the SWAP taxonomy.

Summary of Personality Analysis

Mrs. Palm demonstrates traits of an **obsessional personality** with her structured, controlling, and emotionally detached approach to the conversation.

Johan exhibits a **narcissistic personality** through his grandiosity, self-centeredness, and underlying vulnerability, masked by a confident exterior.

Marianne shows signs of a **dependent-victimized personality**, characterized by her passivity, self-doubt, and reliance on Johan for her identity and self-worth.

This output presents a remarkably insightful and professional analysis of the characters that appear in the first scene of the drama. As a researcher who has been deeply involved in personality analysis and profiling for years (e.g., Neuman, 2016), I would rate the analysis generated by the model very highly. Moreover, the LLM can reflect on its output and propose improvements to the prompt. Therefore, I challenged the model by asking it to reflect and improve:

> Reflect on the output and propose ways of improving the instructions for a better diagnosis.

The model responded as follows:

> Reflecting on the output of the personality analysis, it's clear that, while the analysis provided insights into each participant's personality style, there are several ways the instructions could be improved to gain an even more accurate and nuanced diagnosis. Here are some proposed improvements.
>
> 1. Expand Focus on Contextual and Non-Verbal Cues
>   Current limitation: The analysis relied solely on the spoken words of each participant, without considering the broader context or non-verbal cues that might influence the interpretation of their personalities.
>
>   Improvement: Include instructions to consider the broader context of the conversation, such as the social setting, power dynamics, and possible non-verbal cues (e.g., tone of voice, body language) that could provide additional insights into each participant's personality. For example, Johan's tone when making grandiose statements or Marianne's body language when deferring to Johan could offer deeper insights into their respective personality styles.
> 2. Incorporate Interaction Patterns and Dynamics
>   Current limitation: The analysis primarily focused on individual utterances without fully considering the interaction patterns between participants.

Improvement: Add instructions to analyze the interaction dynamics between participants, such as how they respond to each other, interrupt, or support one another. For example, Johan's interruptions of Marianne and the way she responds could be explored to better understand their relational dynamics and how they reflect their underlying personality styles.

3. Explore Emotional and Cognitive Consistency
   Current limitation: The analysis focused on observable traits without deeply exploring the consistency of emotions and cognitive processes across different parts of the conversation.

   Improvement: Include instructions to assess each participant's emotional and cognitive consistency. For instance, analyze whether Johan's self-praise is consistent throughout the conversation or fluctuates in response to specific prompts, which might indicate underlying insecurities or a complex cognitive process related to his narcissistic personality.

4. Consider the Historical and Relational Background
   Current limitation: The analysis didn't fully account for the participants' historical backgrounds or relational histories, which might influence their current behavior.

   Improvement: Add a step to incorporate the participants' histories, especially the relational history between Johan and Marianne, into the analysis. For example, considering their shared past, as mentioned in the conversation, could provide deeper insights into Marianne's dependency or Johan's grandiosity and show how these traits have evolved.

5. Examine Potential Contradictions or Complexities
   Current limitation: The analysis didn't explicitly look for contradictions or complexities within each participant's behavior that might indicate a more nuanced personality.

   Improvement: Introduce a directive to identify and explore any inconsistencies in the participants' statements or behavior. For example, if Johan expresses grandiosity but also shows moments of vulnerability or self-doubt, this could suggest a more complex narcissistic personality. Similarly, if Marianne occasionally asserts herself, this could indicate internal conflict or evolving personality traits.

6. Incorporate Hypothesis Testing and Alternative Interpretations
   Current limitation: The analysis followed a straightforward approach without considering alternative interpretations or testing different hypotheses.

   Improvement: Encourage hypothesis testing by considering alternative personality styles or traits that might explain certain behaviors. For instance, while Johan's behavior strongly aligns with narcissistic traits, there might be aspects of an obsessional style in his need for control. Testing these hypotheses against the evidence could lead to a more refined diagnosis.

7. Use of a Sliding Window Approach
   Current limitation: The analysis was linear, assessing each participant on the basis of the conversation as a whole.

   Improvement: Implement a sliding window approach where the conversation is broken down into smaller segments for analysis. This would make it possible to identify shifts in behavior or tone that could reveal more about each participant's personality. For instance, analyzing how Marianne's responses change from the beginning to the end of the conversation could provide insights into her emotional state or coping mechanisms.

Conclusion

By incorporating these improvements—focusing on context, interaction patterns, emotional consistency, historical background, contradictions, hypothesis testing, and a sliding window approach—the instructions for diagnosing personality styles using the SWAP taxonomy can become more robust and nuanced. This would lead to a more accurate and comprehensive understanding of each participant's personality, capturing the complexities of human behavior in greater detail.

This shows how reflective the model can be and how it can incorporate our previous 'collaboration' into the improved instructions. Here, I focused on one minor improvement involving the theoretical enrichment of the analysis through another layer of personality analysis. More specifically, I decided to add another external resource of information, a paper describing the idea of *mentalization* (Luyten & Fonagy, 2015). Mentalization refers to the capacity to understand and interpret one's own and others' mental states, such as thoughts, feelings, desires, and intentions. This ability to 'mentalize' is crucial for effective social interaction and emotional regulation, as it allows individuals to make sense of behavior in terms of underlying mental states rather than just external actions. I used this theoretical approach for the next prompt.

PROMPT 7.2

Here is a paper describing the MENTALIZING approach developed by Fonagy.

Use the paper and the mentalization approach to analyze the above conversation.

Generate a professional psychological report analyzing and diagnosing the mentalizing abilities of the participants in the conversation.

END

The model generated the report below.

Psychological Report: Analysis of Mentalizing Abilities in Conversation Participants

Date: [Insert Date]

Participants: Johan, Marianne, Mrs. Palm

Subject: Analysis of Mentalizing Abilities using the Mentalization Approach by Fonagy

Introduction

This psychological report provides an analysis of the mentalizing abilities of the participants in the conversation provided. Fonagy describes mentalizing as the capacity to understand oneself and others through intentional mental states such as feelings, desires, wishes, attitudes, and goals. This analysis will explore how each participant demonstrates—or fails to demonstrate—effective mentalizing in their interactions, using the dimensions of mentalization described in the paper.

Participant 1: **Johan**

Observations

Johan's statements and interactions in the conversation suggest a complex interplay between self-focused and other-focused mentalizing, with potential imbalances that could indicate difficulties in effective mentalization. His initial statement, "I'm not particularly nervous," and his subsequent grandiose self-description ("I'm bright, youthful, successful, and sexy") reflect a strong focus on self-perception and self-presentation, possibly at the expense of accurately mentalizing the perspectives of others.

This is a remarkable observation. Johan is diagnosed as having difficulties in mentalizing the states of others. This explains why he does not understand his wife Marianne and her needs. The model continues with the following analysis.

Analysis

Automatic vs. controlled mentalization: Johan's responses often seem automatic, relying on a rehearsed or reflexive self-presentation. His self-praise appears to be a form of controlled mentalization designed to manage impressions, but it might reflect a deeper reliance on automatic mentalization when under social stress. This could indicate a switch to automatic mentalizing under perceived pressure to maintain his image, which might lead to biased or non-reflective assumptions about the way others view him.

Johan's analysis relies on the difference between automatic and controlled mentalization. A controlled form of mentalization allows us to ponder rationally on the mental states of the self and others rather than respond automatically from the gut. The analysis suggests that under the stress of self-presentation, Johan automatically responds by playing the role of the arrogant joker. Here, we understand that, in contrast with his self-assured presentation, Johan is not the self-assured personality he is trying to sell us. His self is what the insightful psychoanalyst Winnicott described as the false self.

> Self vs. other mentalizing: Johan's focus on self-presentation suggests an over-reliance on self-mentalizing with limited consideration for others' perspectives. His remark about being a 'fantastic lover' and seeking confirmation from Marianne ("Isn't that right, Marianne?") demonstrates a need for validation, indicating potential difficulties in balancing self and other mentalization. This imbalance may lead to a difficulty in accurately perceiving Marianne's mental states and needs.

This layer of mentalization aligns with Johan's previous analysis. Johan seems to be self-centered and ignores the mental states of others. In the film, we can see Marianne's response to his self-description. She seems to be embarrassed. Johan, as a self-centered narcissist, doesn't seem to take Marianne into account when adopting an arrogant stance in front of the journalist.

> Internal vs. external mentalization: Johan's emphasis on external attributes (e.g., youthfulness, success, physical appearance) suggests a stronger orientation towards external mentalization. His mentalization appears to focus on how he is perceived externally, possibly at the expense of internal reflection on his emotional states and their impact on others.
>
> Cognitive vs. affective mentalization: Johan's mentalizing leans more towards cognitive processing—focusing on his achievements and societal roles—than affective mentalization, which involves understanding and reflecting on emotional states. This might indicate a tendency to intellectualize his experiences rather than engage with the underlying emotions.

The model's final conclusion is as follows:

> Johan's mentalizing abilities are characterized by overemphasizing self-focused, external, and cognitive aspects, with potential deficits in accurately understanding others' perspectives and emotions. His mentalizing may be disrupted under stress, leading to automatic, non-reflective responses aimed at preserving his self-image.

This is a remarkably insightful understanding of Johan's narcissistic personality. Next, the model analyzes Marianne. The first observation is this:

> Marianne's contributions to the conversation suggest a more tentative and less assertive approach to mentalizing. Her statements reflect a reliance on external validation and a possible struggle to balance her mental states with those of others, particularly Johan.

The following analysis supports the observation:

Automatic vs. controlled mentalization: Marianne exhibits signs of controlled mentalization, especially in her attempts to present herself in a socially acceptable manner. However, her hesitancy ("What else should I say? This is difficult") indicates that, under stress, she might struggle with maintaining this control, potentially reverting to automatic mentalization, where she defers to Johan's lead.

Self vs. other mentalization: Marianne's mentalizing appears to be other-focused, as seen in her deference to Johan and her concern about how he and Mrs. Palm perceive her. This other-focused approach may lead to difficulties in accurately mentalizing her needs and emotions, as she seems to prioritize Johan's perspective over hers.

Internal vs. external mentalization: Marianne's mentalizing seems to be split between internal and external focus. While she acknowledges her internal state ("I lack Johan's boundless self-assurance"), she also struggles with external mentalization, as shown by her repeated reference to her marriage and children, without expanding on her own personal identity.

Cognitive vs. affective mentalization: Marianne's mentalizing appears to lean towards affect processing, as she expresses emotions like inadequacy and happiness about her life. However, this is often done in a subdued and indirect manner, which might indicate a difficulty in fully integrating cognitive reflections with her affective experiences.

The model concludes like this:

Marianne demonstrates a more affective and other-focused approach to mentalizing, with potential difficulties in self-mentalizing and balancing her internal states with external demands. Her mentalizing abilities might be compromised under stress, leading to reliance on automatic mentalization strategies that prioritize social harmony over personal authenticity.

Observing the drama as a whole, it is striking how insightful the model's conclusion is. The model provides a valid and professional personality analysis of the characters involved in the drama.

Although Mrs. Palm is a minor figure, I asked the model to analyze her forms of mentalization. The model provided the following observations:

As the conversation's facilitator, Mrs. Palm exhibits a controlled and structured approach to mentalizing. Her role as an interviewer requires her to manage the flow of conversation and elicit responses from the participants, which she does directly and professionally.

Here, the model realizes that Mr. Palm's mentalization results from her role/stance and being in charge of the interview. The model provides the following analysis:

Automatic vs. controlled mentalization: Mrs. Palm's mentalizing is predominantly controlled, as she maintains a structured approach to the conversation and intervenes to guide the participants ("Let's move on to the particulars," "Maybe we should talk about your professions"). This suggests a significant capacity for controlled mentalization, with less reliance on automatic, reflexive responses.

Self vs. other mentalizing: Mrs. Palm's mentalizing is other-focused, as her role requires her to understand and manage the mental states of Johan and Marianne. She seems adept at maintaining an objective stance, avoiding deep engagement with her mental states while focusing on facilitating the participants' self-disclosure.

Internal vs. external mentalization: Mrs. Palm effectively balances internal and external mentalization. She is attentive to the external cues provided by the participants (e.g., their verbal responses), while also being aware of the internal dynamics at play (e.g., when Johan makes grandiose statements).

Cognitive vs. affective mentalization: Mrs. Palm's mentalizing is predominantly cognitive, focusing on eliciting information and maintaining the structure of the conversation. There is little evidence of affective engagement, as she maintains a professional and detached demeanor throughout the conversation.

The model ends with this conclusion:

Mrs. Palm demonstrates notable controlled, cognitive, and other-focused mentalizing abilities, which are appropriate for her role as a facilitator. Her ability to manage the conversation and maintain an objective stance suggests a well-developed capacity for mentalization. However, her affective engagement with the participants is minimal, which may be intentional given her role.

The model summarizes with the following analysis:

Johan exhibits an over-reliance on self-focused, external, and cognitive mentalization, with potential difficulties in accurately understanding others' perspectives and managing his emotional states under stress.

Marianne demonstrates a more affective and other-focused approach to mentalization, with challenges in balancing her internal states and asserting her identity in social contexts.

Mrs. Palm shows notable controlled, cognitive, and other-focused mentalization, focusing on managing the conversation rather than engaging emotionally with the participants.

These findings suggest that the mentalizing abilities of the participants are shaped by their roles and personalities, and by the dynamics of their interaction, with varying degrees of effectiveness in understanding and responding to the mental states of themselves and others.

The model provides a highly professional report and would easily pass the Turing test for psychological analysis and diagnosis. At this point, we can sense the AI revolution. The model can analyze the participants in a conversation and provide a highly professional report that would easily compete with the diagnosis of a human expert. We can now imagine an integrated AI model that observes and analyzes a conversation using a multidimensional approach. The model can learn about the participants and their personalities, identify their perspectives in a conversation, and provide insights into the dynamics of the conversation. And when this process is accompanied by the model's metacognitive modules of monitoring, reflection, and regulation, the model can only improve. Given the new AI technologies, the old practices used to understand human behavior are transformed in a quite unprecedented way. At this point, I hope you see why.

HOW DANGEROUS IS JULES?

The final section of this chapter takes a step further by trying to use the LLM to generate a risk assessment of a person using his conversation as data. I used Pulp Fiction and asked the model to analyze the conversation and determine the risk associated with Jules. This may sound like science fiction taken from a novel by Philip K. Dick, but take a look at the model's output and decide for yourself. First, the prompt.

PROMPT 7.3

Analyze the following conversation using the SWAP and the MENTALIZATION approach presented before.

Generate a risk assessment report analyzing the risk of Jules behaving violently.

Generate a professional report and justify your assessment by providing evidence from the conversation.

END

The model generated the following report:

Risk Assessment Report: Analysis of Violent Behavior Risk in Jules

Date: [Insert Date]
Subject: Risk of Violent Behavior in Jules
Participants: Jules, Brett, Vincent, Roger, Marvin

Introduction

This report provides a risk assessment of the potential for violent behavior in the individual named Jules, based on a detailed analysis of the conversation provided. The analysis uses the Shedler–Westen assessment procedure (SWAP) and the mentalization approach developed by Fonagy. The objective is to assess the likelihood of violent behavior and the underlying psychological factors contributing to this risk.

SWAP Analysis

Personality style: **Antisocial-psychopathic personality**

Jules exhibits several characteristics strongly aligned with the antisocial-psychopathic personality style as described by SWAP:

Exploitation and manipulation: Jules tends to exploit and manipulate others, as seen in his interactions with Brett and Roger. He asserts dominance through intimidation, coercing Brett into responding to his questions despite the obvious fear and anxiety he induces.

Lack of remorse: Jules shows no remorse for his violent actions. His shooting of Roger is carried out with a sense of casual indifference, and he immediately resumes his conversation with Brett, mocking his fear and dismissing his previous statements. This lack of remorse or concern for the suffering of others is a hallmark of antisocial psychopathic behavior.

Impulse control: Jules appears to have poor impulse control, as evidenced by his violent outbursts. The abrupt and aggressive manner in which he shoots Roger and later injures Brett suggests a readiness to resort to violence without significant provocation or consideration of consequences.

Grandiosity and sense of superiority: Jules exhibits grandiosity in his interactions, particularly in the way he commands the situation and belittles Brett with remarks like "Check out the big brain on Brett." His sense of superiority is evident in his dismissive and sarcastic responses, further reflecting traits associated with narcissistic tendencies within the antisocial psychopathic spectrum.

The diagnosis provided so far would easily compete with the diagnosis of a professional psychologist or psychiatrist. Next is the analysis based on the mentalization approach.

Mentalization Analysis

Mentalization Impairments and Risk Factors

Automatic vs. controlled mentalization: Jules' behavior is largely governed by automatic mentalization, characterized by reflexive, impulsive responses driven by anger and aggression. His actions, such as shooting Roger and threatening Brett, indicate a reliance on fast, non-reflective processing, particularly under stress. This switch from controlled to automatic mentalization suggests a low threshold for aggression and violence, particularly when he perceives a challenge to his authority or status.

Self vs. other mentalization: Jules demonstrates a strong focus on his own mental states and a marked disregard for those of others. His interactions are centered around his dominance and control, with little or no effort to understand or empathize with the mental states of Brett or Roger. This lack of other-focused mentalization is a significant risk factor for violent behavior, as it reflects an inability or unwillingness to consider the impact of his actions on others.

Cognitive vs. affective mentalization: Jules' mentalizing is predominantly cognitive, focusing on maintaining control and asserting dominance through logical, albeit distorted, reasoning. However, his affective mentalization—understanding and managing emotions—is severely impaired. His actions are driven by intense emotions, such as anger and contempt, but he lacks the capacity to reflect on these emotions in a controlled manner. This imbalance increases the likelihood of violent outbursts when his cognitive strategies fail to maintain control.

Attachment and arousal regulation: Jules' behavior suggests an attachment history that may involve hyperactivation strategies characterized by intense and poorly regulated emotional responses. His readiness to switch to violence under stress indicates a possible history of attachment disruptions that have compromised his ability to regulate arousal effectively. This dysregulation is evident in his quick escalation from verbal intimidation to physical violence, reflecting a breakdown in controlled mentalization under stress.

Based on the above analysis, the model provides the following conclusions and risk assessment:

Based on the SWAP and mentalization analysis, Jules presents a high risk of violent behavior. His personality traits align with the antisocial-psychopathic spectrum, characterized by exploitation, lack of remorse, and poor impulse control. Additionally, his mentalization impairments, particularly his reliance on automatic, self-focused, and cognitively distorted mentalization, further exacerbate the risk of violence.

Key Risk Factors

Impulsivity: Jules' readiness to resort to violence without significant provocation indicates high impulsivity.

Lack of empathy: His disregard for the mental states and suffering of others reduces any internal inhibition against violence.

Attachment dysregulation: Potential attachment issues contribute to his inability to regulate arousal and maintain controlled mentalization, leading to violent outbursts under stress.

The model also provides some recommendations, although I didn't ask it to do so:

Intervention: Given the high risk of violent behavior, immediate intervention is recommended. Strategies should address the underlying attachment issues and improve controlled mentalizing capacities.

Monitoring: Close monitoring of Jules' behavior is necessary, particularly in high-stress situations where his propensity for violence is likely to escalate.

Treatment: Mentalization-based treatment (MBT) may be effective in helping Jules develop better emotional regulation and mentalizing skills, potentially reducing the risk of future violence.

Prepared by: [Your Name]

Title: [Your Title]

Date: [Insert Date]

Signature: [Your Signature]

The above analysis presents a striking ability to understand the personalities involved in a conversation. By supporting the model with external resources relevant to the analysis, it has been attuned to address our specifications and empowered our understanding of the dynamics of a conversation. In the case of Johan and Marianne, we now understand this dynamics as typical of narcissistic and dependent personalities. In the case of *Pulp Fiction*, we now better understand Jules as a dangerous psychopath playing with his prey. The analysis of the characters' personalities converges with the results of the previous analyses. However, one should not make the reductionist mistake of trying to understand the conversation solely through the personalities of the interlocutors. A conversation is a social event, a whole different from the sum of its parts. Understanding the parts, though, may inform our analysis of the whole in a bottom-up and nonlinear way. Being nonlinear by nature, the LLM is an ideal platform for avoiding the reductionist mistake while intelligently analyzing the contribution of the parts.

To conclude, I doubt whether Jules' antisocial personality can be changed in the way recommended by the model. However, there is room for hope. At a certain point, Jules experiences redemption, believing that God saved his life. He decides to change, and when he encounters Honey Bunny and Pumpkin, he spares their lives in an unusual move that indicates that he has genuinely changed. This shift in the plot shows how uncertain life is and how social dynamics may surprise us even when we know its components.

SUMMARY

- Understanding the personalities of the participants in a conversation is crucial as it frames their interactions and influences the conversational dynamics.
- LLMs can effectively diagnose personality styles when prompted with specific frameworks like SWAP or mentalization analysis.
- This chapter suggests ways to refine LLM prompts by including external resources.
- The analysis of conversations using LLMs can also extend to assessing the risk of violent behavior by identifying personality traits associated with antisocial or psychopathic tendencies.
- Using the above approach, we have better-understood conversations from *Pulp Fiction* and *Scenes from a Marriage*.

REFERENCES

Luyten, P., & Fonagy, P. (2015). The neurobiology of mentalizing. *Personality Disorders: Theory, Research, and Treatment, 6*(4), 366.

Neuman, Y. (2016). *Shakespeare for the Intelligence Agent: Toward Understanding Real Personalities.* Lanham, MD: Rowman & Littlefield.

Neuman, Y., & Cohen, Y. (2024). A data set of synthetic utterances for computational personality analysis. *Scientific Data, 11*(1), 623.

Westen, D., Shedler, J., Bradley, B., & DeFife, J. A. (2012). An empirically derived taxonomy for personality diagnosis: Bridging science and practice in conceptualizing personality. *American Journal of Psychiatry, 169*(3), 273–284.

8

HOW AI CAN READ FLIRTATION, AMBIGUITY, AND COHERENCE

"I AM NOT FLIRTING WITH YOU"

Conversations are not just a medium for exchanging information. They are also playgrounds characterized by complexity, ambiguity, incoherence, and double binds where one says one thing and means another. Flirting is just one example illustrating this complex aspect of language. Previously, I analyzed a conversation in *Scenes from a Marriage*. To recall, the model interpreted Katarina's exchange with Johan as flirting. However, I didn't focus on this aspect of the conversation, which illustrates language in its complexity. Here, I show how large language models (LLMs) can analyze flirtation by considering the inherent ambiguity in a conversation.

Flirting is a social interaction involving verbal and non-verbal signals to communicate interest, attraction, or playful intent toward another person. It often includes teasing, compliments, light-hearted jokes, eye contact, body language, and subtle touches. Flirting is typically characterized by its playful and somewhat *ambiguous* nature, where the intent may not be explicitly stated, leaving room for interpretation. Why ambiguity? To save the face of the flirting individual, if necessary. For instance, imagine an individual expressing

DOI: 10.1201/9781003591047-8

unambiguous interest in a woman. The woman acknowledges his interest but responds with denial. She herself has no interest in the individual. According to the theory of emotions presented previously, this rejection may be interpreted in terms of a valuation: her rejection means that she doesn't value the individual highly enough. Such an interpretation could be taken to imply a face-threatening act because the individual might experience devaluation, which could then result in anger. However, if the man is flirting and his interest is ambiguous, it will not be clear whether he is interested or not, and a rejection need not be seen to threaten his face. He can save face by denying that he had any real interest.

Understanding flirtation may help us to better understand some of the more complex mechanisms involved in a conversation and the way people make sense of conversations. To address this challenge, I analyze a thin slice of an interaction in Silver Linings Playbook and then go on to study coherence in another conversation. Why flirtation and coherence? Ambiguity is one way of violating coherence, and when coherence is violated, the way is open to different interpretations. Complexity emerges in a conversation when several interpretations are possible. I will present these points by showing how LLM can be prompted to identify these deeper layers of human conversation.

Silver Linings Playbook is a romantic comedy-drama film. It stars Bradley Cooper as Pat Solitano, a man suffering from a mental disorder who, after being released from a psychiatric hospital, tries to reconcile with his wife, who betrayed him. Jennifer Lawrence plays Tiffany Maxwell, a young widow with her own issues, who offers to help Pat to recommunicate with his wife if he'll be her dance partner for an upcoming competition.

Pat and Tiffany are first introduced when invited to dinner at Ronnie's house. He is Pat's best friend and married to Tiffany's sister. Pat has just learned that Tiffany lost her husband but does not know how. He is curious to know how, but Tiffany enters, and he cannot get the information from Ronnie. Norms of politeness are such that Pat cannot satisfy his curiosity with respect to Tifffany's dead husband. The first exchange between Pat and Tiffany is as follows:

Pat:	You look nice.
Tiffany:	Thank you.
Pat:	I'm not flirting with you.
Tiffany:	Oh, I didn't think you were.
Pat:	I just see that you made an effort and I'm gonna be better with my wife, I'm working on that. I wanna acknowledge her beauty. I never used to do that. I do that now. 'Cause we're gonna be better than ever...Nikki. Just practicing. How'd Tommy die?

Have a look at Pat's last utterance. It is disproportionately long. Does that signal something? Let us analyze the conversation using the model, paying attention to more complex layers of the utterances. As we have already done, we start with speech acts.

Pat *compliments* Tiffany, saying that she looks nice. Tiffany responds to this speech act of complimenting by expressing her *gratitude*. This is a common pattern of speech acts: a compliment is responded to with gratitude or acknowledgment. It is a common pattern of polite conversation. Surprisingly, Pat asserts that he is not flirting with Tiffany. His utterance deviates from a common conversation pattern as it attempts to correct a possible impression formed by his compliment. However, it is unclear whether Tiffany or any of the hosts would have considered Pat's compliment as an act of flirtation. Pat's utterance, followed by his assertion, indicates that his first utterance is ambivalent, at least for him, and it can be interpreted as a compliment per se or as a compliment that is in fact flirtatious. Pat's response exposes the ambiguity of his utterance. Tiffany's response suggests that the ambiguity is *idiosyncratic* and exists only in Pat's mind. We can see that ambiguity is not necessarily objective. It may exist only for some of the participants in a conversation. The answer to the question of "ambiguous for whom?" may inform us about the participants and their dynamics.

To better understand ambiguity in language, we may use the LLM to draw on external resources and to look for the most up-to-date knowledge about research on ambiguity. We could direct the model to Wikipedia's entry on ambiguity,[1] but we can also use advanced tools for research. Current AI technologies may direct us to up-to-date and validated sources of knowledge. For example, STORM[2] is a new tool developed by Stanford University. The tool applies "large language models to write grounded and organized long-form articles from scratch, with comparable breadth and depth to Wikipedia pages" (Shao et al., 2024, p. 1). We can use the tool to produce an up-to-date knowledge source on ambiguity. However, the tool has another advantage. It can take into account the context of your task. I explained the context as follows:

> I would like to use a large language model to identify ambiguous utterances in a conversation. I am seeking knowledge to help me prompt the LLM for this task.

STORM created a nine-page article dealing with ambiguity. Armed with this knowledge, I returned to the model to explore its ability to identify ambiguity in a conversation.

CAN LLMs IDENTIFY AMBIGUITY?

To explore the model's ability to identify ambiguity, I used a conversation from *Night at the Opera* (1935).[3] This is one of the Marx brothers' most famous and hilarious comedies. The plot involves Otis B. Driftwood (played by Groucho Marx), who is trying to 'help' a wealthy widow, Mrs. Claypool, break into high society by investing in the opera. Along the way, he encounters two other Marx Brothers, Fiorello (Chico Marx) and Tomasso (Harpo Marx), helping their friend, a struggling tenor named Ricardo, to get a break in the opera world. The scene I analyze is *The Contract Scene*.

In this scene, Driftwood sets up a meeting for Mrs. Claypool with Herman Gottlieb, the director of the New York Opera Company. Gottlieb is also interested in Mrs. Claypool's money, but in a more respectable way than Driftwood. He convinces her to pay for an arrogant tenor named Rodolfo Lassparri to sing in New York. Driftwood sees a chance to make money from this deal and tries to sign Lassparri first. Along the way, he meets Fiorello, who has his tenor, Riccardo Baroni, to promote. That's when the real fun begins…. Here is a slice from the conversation:

Driftwood:	Oh I know, I know, the greatest tenor in the world. That's what I'm after.
Fiorello:	Why, I'm his manager!
Driftwood:	Who's manager?
Fiorello:	The greatest tenor in the world!
Driftwood:	The fella that sings at the opera here?!
Fiorello:	Sure.
Driftwood:	What's his name?
Fiorello:	What-a-you care, I can't pronounce it. What do you want with him?
Driftwood:	I wanted to sign him up for the New York Opera Company. Do you know America is waiting to hear him sing!?
Fiorello:	Well…He can sing loud but he can't sing that loud.

I focus on the last two utterances of the conversation. Driftwood mistakes Fiorello for the manager of the famous opera singer Lassparri and wants to sign the singer. He says, "America is waiting to hear him singing," to which Fiorello replies, "he can't sing that loud." The ambiguity in this exchange results from Fiorello's misinterpretation of Driftwood's utterance. When Driftwood says that America is waiting to hear him singing, he doesn't mean it literally. However, his utterance can be interpreted, which is what Fiorello is doing. The humor results from Fiorello's misinterpretation.

We may ask whether the model is intelligent enough to identify the ambiguity, the misinterpretation of the utterance, and its resulting effect in terms of humor. To prompt the model, I first gave it the article produced by STORM.

PROMPT 8.1

Theoretical background: [STORM'S ARTICLE HERE]
Task: Analyzing Ambiguous Utterances in a Conversation
Subtasks:

1. **Identify Ambiguous Utterances**
    Identify any utterances in the conversation provided that possess multiple possible interpretations.
2. **Explain Potential Interpretations**
    For each ambiguous utterance identified, list and explain the different possible interpretations. Ensure that both the literal and any figurative or humorous interpretations are considered.
3. **Assess the Reasonableness of the Interpretations**
    Evaluate which interpretation is the most reasonable based on the context of the conversation. Consider the tone, intention, and character dynamics when making this judgment.
4. **Determine the Addressee's Interpretation**
    Analyze how the addressee (the person the utterance is directed to) appears to interpret the ambiguous utterance. Provide evidence from the subsequent dialogue or actions that support your conclusion.
5. **Examine the Impact of a Less Reasonable Interpretation**
    If the addressee adopts a less reasonable interpretation, explain how this affects the conversation. Consider how this misinterpretation might influence the dynamics, tone, or outcome of the interaction.

##

The context of the conversation is: [INSERT THE DESCRIPTION HERE]
The conversation is: [CONVERSATION HERE]
END

The model produced the following analysis:

Task: Analyzing Ambiguous Utterances in a Conversation
Subtask 1: Identify Ambiguous Utterances

The ambiguous utterance in the conversation is: "Well…He can sing loud but he can't sing that loud."

Subtask 2: Explain Potential Interpretations

1. **Literal interpretation**: Fiorello suggests that while the tenor has a loud voice, it's not powerful enough to be heard all the way from Europe (where they currently are) in America, thus making it impossible for America to hear him sing.

2. **Figurative/humorous interpretation**: Fiorello is humorously implying that although the tenor has a loud voice, it is not metaphorically or symbolically grand enough to make a significant impact or to be heard in the metaphorical sense, such as becoming famous in America.

We can see that the model somehow missed the humor.

Subtask 3: Assess Reasonableness of Interpretations

The **humorous interpretation** is the most reasonable in this context, given the comedic nature of the scene and the personalities involved. The conversation between Driftwood and Fiorello is filled with quick-witted banter, suggesting that Fiorello's comment is intended to be humorous rather than taken literally.

Subtask 4: Determine the Addressee's Interpretation

Driftwood's interpretation: Driftwood likely understands the humorous intent behind Fiorello's statement. However, the ambiguity could lead Driftwood to consider the literal impossibility momentarily before recognizing the joke. This is consistent with the style of humor in the scene, where one character makes a humorous comment and the other plays along, maintaining the comedic flow.

Subtask 5: Examine the Impact of a Less Reasonable Interpretation

If Driftwood were to adopt the **literal interpretation**, the humor would be lost, and the conversation might take a more serious or absurd turn, deviating from the intended comedic effect. This misinterpretation could make the interaction awkward, as it would disrupt the playful banter and potentially lead to a misunderstanding about the tenor's abilities, shifting the scene's tone from lighthearted to confusing.

Conclusion

The ambiguity in Fiorello's statement enhances the scene's comedic nature, emphasizing the dual meanings of 'loud' and the exaggerated idea that a voice could be heard across an ocean. The most reasonable interpretation within the context is the humorous one, which both maintains the flow of the conversation and contributes to the overall comedic effect of the dialogue.

We can see that the model can identify ambiguity when directed through the relevant resources, but it is mistaking some factual information. For example, it believes the conversation took place in Europe. This reminds us that the model is not perfect, but who is …?

When applying the same prompt to the exchange between Pat and Tiffany, we get the following output:

Task: Analyzing Ambiguous Utterances in a Conversation
Subtask 1: Identify Ambiguous Utterances

The ambiguous utterance in the conversation is: "I'm not flirting with you."

Here is another mistake. The ambiguous utterance is the first utterance in the conversation, not "I'm not flirting with you." However, this mistake is corrected in the next output.

Subtask 2: Explain Potential Interpretations

1. **Literal interpretation**: Pat directly clarifies that his compliment ("You look nice") was not intended as a flirtatious remark. He wants to ensure Tiffany understands that his intentions are not romantic or suggestive.

   Here, the model correctly identifies the utterance as defensive. Moreover, the model correctly analyzes the utterance as involving overcompensation:

2. **Defensive interpretation**: Pat might be trying to defend himself preemptively, assuming that Tiffany might misinterpret his compliment as flirting, even though she hasn't indicated any such assumption.

3. **Overcompensating interpretation**: Pat's statement could also imply that he is overcompensating for his feelings of guilt regarding his relationship with his wife, Nikki. By explicitly stating he's not flirting, he might be trying to convince himself more than Tiffany that his intentions are purely innocent.

When assessing the reasonableness of the interpretation, the model correctly identifies the defensive aspect, as we now see.

Subtask 3: Assess Reasonableness of Interpretations
The **defensive interpretation** is the most reasonable given the context. Pat's immediate follow-up statement suggests that he is overly concerned about how Tiffany might perceive his compliment. This concern likely stems from his insecurities or the need to reassure himself of his commitment to his wife.

Previously, and following Holquist, I emphasized the importance of the response for understanding meaning. This point becomes clear when the model analyzes Tiffany's response.

Subtask 4: Determine the Addressee's Interpretation
Tiffany's interpretation: Tiffany seems to interpret Pat's statement as unnecessary and perhaps a bit awkward, as indicated by her response, "Oh, I didn't think you were." This suggests

that she didn't perceive his compliment as flirtatious and was not expecting such a clarification. Her calm and straightforward reaction shows she took his words at face value without overthinking them.

Finally, the model analyzes another deep aspect of Tiffany's response and concludes.

Subtask 5: Examine the Impact of a Less Reasonable Interpretation

If Tiffany had interpreted Pat's statement as **overcompensating**, she might have questioned his intentions further or felt uncomfortable, sensing that Pat was struggling with his feelings. This could have introduced tension into the conversation, potentially making Tiffany feel awkward or leading her to doubt Pat's sincerity. However, since Tiffany does not react this way, the conversation remains on a relatively even keel, albeit with some underlying tension due to Pat's evident discomfort.

Conclusion

The ambiguity in Pat's statement, "I'm not flirting with you," reflects his internal struggle and defensiveness. While he might be trying to clarify his intentions, the statement introduces an element of awkwardness, which Tiffany handles by downplaying the situation. The most reasonable interpretation is that Pat is being defensive, trying to preempt any possible misunderstanding, but in doing so, he inadvertently highlights his insecurities.

While the model fails in some aspects, the bottom line of its analysis is valid. It identifies Pat's inner struggle and defensiveness and points out his awkward behavior.

COHERENCE AND INCOHERENCE

Ambiguity may result in a break in the coherence of the conversation. Coherence refers to the question of whether the different pieces of a text fit together. If an utterance is ambiguous, it may impede the flow of the conversation and its coherence. I provided the model with the following prompt to identify incoherence in a text and asked it to analyze the short exchange between Pat and Tiffany.

PROMPT 8.2

Analyzing Coherence and Incoherence in Conversations

> Task: Analyze the following conversation to identify utterances expressing incoherence. Use the theoretical background to evaluate the coherence of the conversation, focusing on the following subtasks:

> Identify utterances expressing incoherence: Highlight any parts of the conversation where the flow of ideas is disrupted, where there is a lack of logical progression, or where the topic shifts abruptly without appropriate transitions.

> Analyze the causes of incoherence: Use concepts from the theoretical background (e.g., logical flow, thematic consistency, transitional devices) to explain why these utterances disrupt the coherence of the conversation.

> Evaluate the impact on the conversation: Assess how the identified incoherence affects the overall conversation, particularly regarding participant understanding, engagement, and the smooth progression of the dialogue.

> Conversation for analysis: [CONVERSATION HERE]
> END

The model analyzed this as follows:

Task: Analyzing Coherence in a Conversation
Subtask 1: Identify Utterances Expressing Incoherence
In the conversation provided, the following utterance by Pat expresses incoherence:

Pat: "I just see that you made an effort and I'm gonna be better with my wife, I'm working on that. I wanna acknowledge her beauty. I never used to do that. I do that now. 'Cause we're gonna be better than ever... Nikki. Just practicing. How'd Tommy die?"

The model correctly identified the last utterance as incoherent. As you remember, I opened the chapter by pointing out the length of Pat's utterance and questioning its meaning. Here, the model identifies some incoherence in the utterance and explains it as follows:

Subtask 2: Explain the Incoherence

1. **Lack of logical flow**: Pat's statement begins with a reflection on Tiffany's appearance and then abruptly shifts to discussing his efforts to improve his relationship with his wife, Nikki. The transition from acknowledging Tiffany's efforts to improving his relationship with Nikki is somewhat disconnected and lacks a logical progression. This shift is confusing because it introduces a new topic (his marriage) without a proper transition from the previous one (Tiffany's appearance).

2. **Sudden topic shift**: The most incoherent aspect of Pat's utterance is the abrupt transition from discussing his marriage and self-improvement to asking how Tommy died. There is no clear connection between these topics, making the shift jarring and potentially confusing for Tiffany. This sudden change disrupts the flow of the conversation, leaving the listener to make sense of the non-sequitur.

3. **Contextual misalignment**: The conversation starts with a polite exchange, then quickly turns to Pat's personal reflections on his marriage, and finally jumps to a serious and unrelated topic about someone's death. This misalignment of topics within a short span creates a sense of incoherence, as it lacks thematic consistency and fails to build logically on the previous statements.

Following the idea that meaning is revealed by response, we can benefit from assessing the impact of Pat's incoherence.

Subtask 3: Assess the Impact of the Incoherence

Impact on the conversation: The incoherence in Pat's speech likely creates confusion and discomfort for Tiffany. The sudden shift in topics can leave her unsure how to respond or to interpret Pat's intentions. This can hinder the natural flow of the conversation, making it difficult for Tiffany to engage meaningfully. The abruptness of the question about Tommy's death, following a seemingly unrelated comment on Pat's marriage, might also create emotional discomfort or awkwardness, further disrupting the coherence of the interaction.

The model concludes the analysis by saying:

The incoherence in Pat's utterances arises from sudden topic shifts, lack of logical flow, and contextual misalignment. These factors disrupt the coherence of the conversation, making it challenging for Tiffany to follow or respond effectively. Understanding these elements is crucial for identifying and addressing incoherence in communication, and ensuring that conversations remain clear, engaging, and contextually appropriate.

The model's conclusions clearly identify Pat as the source of incoherence. The identification of ambiguities and breaks in coherence is informative about the participants and the dynamics of the conversation. It is not accidental that the model identified Pat as the source of the disorder. Pat tries to clarify what he conceives as ambiguity and breaks the conversation, showing no tact. Luckily, things improve, and at the end of the movie, Pat and Tiffany experience love and redemption.

Applying the same prompt to the exchange from *Night at the Opera*, we get this:

1. Identify Utterances Expressing Incoherence
   The utterance by Fiorello: "Well...He can sing loud but he can't sing that loud."

To recall, the model failed to identify the utterance as ambiguous but now succeeds in identifying it as incoherent. Moreover, it explains the incoherence as follows:

2. Analyze the Causes of Incoherence
   Logical flow: The conversation initially follows a logical flow, with Driftwood expressing interest in signing a great

tenor for the New York Opera Company and Fiorello engaging in the exchange by claiming to be the tenor's manager.
However, the coherence is disrupted when Fiorello responds
to Driftwood's excitement about America's anticipation with
the comment, "Well…He can sing loud, but he can't sing that
loud." This response introduces incoherence because it disrupts the expected progression of the conversation. Instead of
providing more details about the tenor or engaging further in
the negotiation, **Fiorello shifts to a humorous remark that
is not directly connected to the logical flow of ideas**.

The model identifies the utterance as incoherent because it shifts
the conversation to a humorous frame. This point is now further
explained.

> Transitional devices: The transition between Driftwood's state-
> ment about America's eagerness to hear the tenor sing and
> Fiorello's response lacks coherence. Fiorello's comment does
> not build upon Driftwood's excitement but rather introduces
> a comedic element that shifts the conversation away from its
> thematic focus on the tenor's potential success.
>
> Contextual misalignment: The humor in Fiorello's statement is
> contextually jarring. While the conversation had been rela-
> tively straightforward up to that point, with both characters
> discussing the tenor's potential, Fiorello's remark about the
> tenor's volume suddenly introduces an exaggerated, almost
> absurd element that misaligns with the context of a serious
> business negotiation. This creates a disjointed moment in
> the conversation.

Below, we see that the impact on the conversation is the most
important element of the analysis (emphasis mine).

> 3. Evaluate the Impact on the Conversation
> Impact on understanding: Fiorello's response, while humor-
> ous, *might cause confusion for Driftwood or the audience if taken literally.*
> The sudden shift to humor disrupts the serious tone of the

conversation, potentially leading to a momentary *breakdown in communication*. This unexpected and incongruent remark could momentarily derail Driftwood's focus on signing the tenor.

Engagement and flow: The engagement in the conversation may suffer due to this incoherent shift. While the humor may entertain, it does not contribute to the progression of the conversation's primary goal (negotiating the tenor's contract). This disruption could hinder the characters' effective exchange of information and intentions.

The model suggests how the coherence could have been improved.

4. Propose Strategies for Enhancing Coherence
    Logical sequencing: Fiorello could maintain coherence by responding in a way that directly addresses Driftwood's excitement about America's anticipation. For example, instead of making a humorous remark, Fiorello could have said something like, "He's definitely the loudest voice you'll hear, but I'm not sure if he's ready for New York just yet." This response would maintain the logical flow and keep the conversation aligned with the topic.

    Use of transitional devices: Introducing transitional phrases that connect the humor to the context could help maintain coherence. Fiorello could say, "Well, he can sing loud, but I guess we'll need more than just volume to impress New York!" This transition acknowledges the humor but also ties it back to the serious topic of the negotiation.

    Contextual alignment: Keeping the humor aligned with the context of the conversation could prevent incoherence. For instance, a comment like, "He's got the voice for it, but we'll need to work on his stage presence," would introduce humor without disrupting the flow of the negotiation.

The model finally concludes:

The conversation between Driftwood and Fiorello exhibits a moment of incoherence due to a sudden *shift in tone and a lack of logical progression*. By understanding the causes of this incoherence, such as the disruption in logical flow and contextual misalignment, strategies can be implemented to maintain coherence in future interactions. This approach ensures that the conversation remains engaging, clear, and focused on its primary objectives.

The model, although imperfect, can identify complex aspects of conversations, such as ambiguity and coherence, and interpret them from a pragmatic perspective. This ability is of huge significance for understanding human conversations in various contexts. A student of mine, deep into the Asperger's spectrum, shared his frustrating experience with dating. I suggested that he work on a project where a model helps an Asperger to date by training him to understand ambiguities and coherence. By working on this project, he was able to better understand himself and found some ways of improving his dating experiences. AI agents could assist Aspergers with dating by mediating the complexities and nuances of social life to those who find them less trivial to understand.

SUMMARY

- Ambiguity allows for multiple interpretations of utterances.
- Flirting often involves playful ambiguity, which can mask coherence and lead to different interpretations, making conversations more complex and dynamic.
- LLMs can effectively identify and analyze pragmatic ambiguities in conversations, providing insights into the underlying social dynamics and the participants' intentions.
- LLMs can also identify and explain incoherence in a conversation.
- The model's ability to identify ambiguity and incoherence can help us to understand conversations and perhaps provide support for the social interactions of those who have difficulties in understanding conversations.

NOTES

1 https://en.m.wikipedia.org/wiki/Ambiguity
2 https://storm.genie.stanford.edu/
3 https://en.wikipedia.org/wiki/A_Night_at_the_Opera_(film)

REFERENCE

Shao, Y., Jiang, Y., Kanell, T. A., Xu, P., Khattab, O., & Lam, M. S. (2024). *Assisting in writing Wikipedia-like articles from scratch with large language models.* arXiv preprint arXiv:2402.14207.

9

FINAL COMMENTS

WHAT HAVE WE LEARNED FROM THIS BOOK?

Understanding others is a constant challenge in our lives as social beings. Therefore, it is not surprising that researchers have analyzed human interactions, language use, and meaning-making (e.g., Voloshinov, 1986; Clark, 1996; Becker, 2000; Hoey, 2012/2013) using various methodologies (e.g., Antaki, 2008). These studies have contributed to our understanding by providing us with conceptual and theoretical tools for framing human conversations. But they were limited in many other respects, as can be expected from any set of tools. Naturally, therefore, at a certain point in the history of analyzing human interactions, there came a moment when little further progress could be made. Indeed, as I have long been involved in this kind of research on language and social interactions, I can testify that not much new has been achieved in this field for at least 20 years. What you see is always more of the same. The old creeks seem to have been blocked up, and nothing now flows out. In natural systems, such blockages are usually circumvented by paving new ways rather than trying to dig out the old routes. And the AI revolution is indeed an opportunity to pave new ways rather than continue the same old practices.

There are several ways in which new technologies can revolutionize our understanding of language use. The first is the

DOI: 10.1201/9781003591047-9

complexity with which sequences can be represented and analyzed. The old ways of representing language use sometimes emphasized simplicity over validity. This means that the old explanations, such as Kintsch's approach to comprehension, emphasize the simplicity of the scientific models over their explanatory power. A simple explanation is appealing, but we may need a better approach to understand a complex system. For example, as I explained earlier, OpenAI uses embeddings of very high dimensionality to represent the meanings of words. Meaning is represented in a way that goes beyond our limited ability to visualize and communicate. Can you explain the meaning of a sentence represented through embeddings in more than 3000 dimensions? Probably not. And yet, this form of representation works, and it works extremely well.

The reason is that embeddings are able to represent crucial aspects of meaning. First, meaning has a probabilistic distributional structure, as anticipated by the pioneering work of Zelig Harris (1954). The mathematics of large language models (LLMs) is not as Chomsky imagined. Sequences are processed as probabilistic patterns. Moreover, the sequences are processed by adjusting the units to each other to allow the LLMs to represent context. This means that the issue of context essential to our understanding of language use (e.g., Becker, 2000) has finally found its place in AI (Neuman, 2024). The probabilistic aspect of LLMs supports their ability to guess the next token in a sequence. These models can therefore represent meanings in their full complexity, present context sensitivity, and make successful predictions. LLMs are the true revolution, but other AI tools empower this revolution. For example, memory-supporting systems allow the model to keep track of the past and adjust itself to the particularity of the user. While an LLM is trained by single-shot learning, there are ways of tuning it to specific cases and there are new technologies that support it with memory so that it may remain sensitive to the particularity of a previous interaction.

This property is very similar to what is actually observed in the natural world. The brain is the general machinery with which we are all equipped at birth. But brains differ because the kind of memory we inherit is different for different species. My brain thus differs from the brain of my cats. My brain also differs from the brain of my reader because we carry different memories. Throughout our lives, we collect experiences and memories that shape our individuality. We are who we are precisely because of these particularities. The ability of LLMs to include a memory component brings them closer to the way human beings think and interact with each other.

LLMs can also consult and exploit various external resources. When studying any given topic, I consult external resources, such as Wikipedia and the Web. Similarly, LLMs can also access these external and regularly updated sources of knowledge. As an experienced learner, I may also learn to reflect on my thoughts and actions in order to improve them. LLMs can do the same. They can examine their moves in constructive ways and get better. Finally, LLMs are not only question-answering machines. They can interact with us sequentially through a series of moves and maintain interactions with one or more agents. These agents can be human agents or a group of artificial agents with whom they converse and work. These abilities go far beyond what we have known so far.

In this short book, I have presented the relevance of LLMs for understanding human conversations. Hopefully, it will be clear how LLMs can provide a deep and real-time analysis of an ongoing conversation. I have argued that human expertise combined with the power of the models is the key to this understanding. Like a good mentor, the human expert may guide the model to perform extremely well and vice versa. The secret sauce of this synergetic approach is the prompting. A human prompting the model is not just someone asking a question; it is someone actually *mediating* the machine's thinking process. Similarly, the machine is not simply an input–output device but a tool humans can use to *mediate* their own thinking process. I have illustrated this approach with various examples, from how to understand the dynamics of a married couple to ambiguity in humor and coherence in a conversation. The reader has thus been equipped with a powerful new approach and numerous illustrations of the way appropriate prompts can get mind and machine to work together.

REFERENCES

Antaki, C. (2008). Discourse analysis and conversation analysis. In P. Alasuutari, L. Bickman, J. Brannen (Eds.), *The SAGE Handbook of Social Research Methods*, pp. 431–447. NY: Sage.

Becker, A. L. (2000). *Beyond Translation: Essays toward a Modern Philology*. Michigan, MI: University of Michigan Press.

Clark, H. H. (1996). *Using Language*. Cambridge: Cambridge University Press.

Harris, Z. S. (1954). Distributional structure. *Word*, 10(2–3), pp. 146–162.

Hoey, M. (2012). *Lexical Priming: A New Theory of Words and Language*. London: Routledge.

Hoey, M. (2013). *Textual Interaction: An Introduction to Written Discourse Analysis*. London: Routledge.

Neuman, Y. (2024). *AI for Understanding Context*. New York, NY: Springer-Nature.

Voloshinov, V. N. (1986). *Marxism and the Philosophy of Language*. Boston, MA: Harvard University Press.

INDEX

For Product Safety Concerns and Information please contact our EU representative GPSR@taylorandfrancis.com
Taylor & Francis Verlag GmbH, Kaufingerstraße 24, 80331 München, Germany